Clarice has put together a wonderful mix of wisdom and wonder for those of us lucky enough to be grandparents. This book helps grandparents be intentional in their role giving that role a richer and deeper meaning which is certain to benefit all children...and all our futures.

Nebraska's Head Football Coach
Tom Osborne and his wife Nancy
Grandparents

...the wisdom of Clarice Orr is so "on target"...Her warmth and sincerity shine through as she shares an extremely important message about savoring the grandparenting experience. Her "from the heart" approach will touch your heart.

Cathy Blythe
Morning Show Co-Host
KFOR Radio, Lincoln, Nebraska

...truly an inspiration and filling a very important need...a wonderful mission.

Marjorie Holmes
America's favorite inspirational writer

"THE JOY OF GRANDPARENTING"
... A WINNER.

Bil KEANE
GRANDFATHER OF 8.

The Joy of Grandparenting

Grandparents Make A Difference

*Grandparents sprinkle
stardust in our lives!*

Clarice Carlson Orr

Clarice Carlson Orr

Dageforde Publishing

10 9 8 7 6 5 4 3 2 1
ISBN #: 1-886225-00-1
Library of Congress Catalog Number: 95-67533

Cover Design by Angie Johnson Art Productions.

Printed in United States of America.

Dageforde Publishing
941 'O' Street, Suite 728
Lincoln, Nebraska 68508-3625
(402) 475-1123

he *Joy of Grandparenting* is dedicated to my children and their spouses — John and Marilyn Orr, Cheryle and Lou Paglialonga, Cyndi and Doug Parrott, and Becky and Nick Reisinger — who have made me a grandmother. My step-grandchildren and step-great-grandchildren give me another perspective that enriches my life. For my best laboratory experience my heart is overflowing with gratitude and joy to my ten grandchildren — Alex, Patrick, Michael, Claire, Emilie, Phillip, Carrie, Matthew, Mark, John and Tanya, my granddaughter-in-law who adds a new dimension to the family.

Let LOVE hover over these pages
and come to nest, gently and warmly,
in the hearts of those who read these words.

Table of Contents

Foreword

The grandparenting movement in America has been gathering force for the past three decades. It is a grass roots movement that began as a simultaneous consciousness in the hearts and minds of a diversity of people living all over the country. Over the years these ideas have expanded and spread. Today the importance of grandparenting is beginning to be recognized by over seventy million American grandparents and society, in general.

Decades ago Clarice Orr raised the beacon of grandparenting in the heartland of America. My wife Carol and I came to know Clarice as a colleague, educator and friend at the time she was engaged in her pioneering efforts in her home state of Nebraska to teach grandparents about the "Joy of Grandparenting." Although she didn't know it at the time Clarice was creating the foundation for a nationwide effort in grandparent education. Today, her educational efforts are being carried on by a new generation of teachers, clinicians and researchers in communities, schools, colleges and religious and government institutions.

In the recent past Clarice has proceeded to expand her work to the field of academic research, nationally, as a social advocate of the grandparenting cause, and now as an author. With this book *The Joy of Grandparenting: Grandparents Make A Difference* she has taken a further step to teach and share her wisdom and experience about grandparents, parents and grandchildren.

What I find exceptional about this book is its usefulness. Written in a warm and intimate style, it is a mine of everyday down-to-earth, common sense and how-to information about the roles, functions and importance of grandparenting. In addition Clarice, because she realistically recognizes potential pitfalls of family life, offers good advice for dealing with adverse situations. Simply put, the book teaches about enhancing the positives of grandparenting while, at the same time, gives sage counsel about eliminating personal or familial roadblocks to being an effective grandparent.

This book is a must read for people who understand the profound importance of the grandparenting role as a life stage and how involved elders can benefit their families, community and nation. Furthermore the book makes it clear that grandparenting, as a role and function is linked to living a fulfilling and meaningful old age. The book teaches how, by being a joyful grandparent, the reader can make a positive emotional, social and spiritual difference in the lives of their children, grandchildren and great-grandchildren and create a legacy that will live after them in the hearts and souls of their issue.

Arthur Kornhaber, M.D.
Founder of the Foundation for Grandparenting

Preface

here is joy in grandparenting. Some people study it, some write about it, some avoid it; most of us who have grandchildren live it.

In the following pages, Clarice Orr offers her well-researched ideas — through thesis and experience — for grandparenting to those of us who became grandparents when we weren't looking.

Grandparenting is a lot like becoming a parent for the first time. There are no rules, no regulations, no guidelines. And grandparenting, too, is learned by doing. The difference is that someone else is ultimately responsible for the child's welfare.

Grandparenting validates your role as a parent. Nothing is more fulfilling than a daughter calling you for suggestions on parenting that little one they just brought home from the hospital or the four year old who knows more than most teens.

A plaque given to me for my first Mother's Day hangs above my computer desk. "Grandmas are for loving and hugging." That's what grandmas do best: They hug and they love. They babysit; they offer suggestions; they hold hands; they go to ballgames, concerts and

Sunday School programs. Grandmas have big shoes to fill.

Grandpas do, too. And great-grandpas and grandmas. I watch with joy as Grandpa pushes our granddaughter on the swing hanging from the maple tree in the back yard. Kelsey and Papa made the swing from a rope and a board — together. Papa watches Kelsey as she begs to go higher and higher. "I **really** love this swing, Papa," she squeals. It brings back fond memories of his childhood when his maternal grandfather built him a swing in the yard on the family farm. Taking time to be a grandparent is important to both the child and the grandparent. It builds lasting bonds and wonderful memories.

As you read this book, keep in mind that we are grandparents together. Each of us has a role to play in that special child's life. Clarice helps us determine our roles and put that Joy in Grandparenting.

Linda J. Dageforde, Grandmother
Editor and Publisher

"I'm not prejudiced, some of my best friends are grandparents."

aving studied textbooks, research journals, popular magazines and books concerning grandparenthood, I call myself a professional grandmother. However, this book really was compiled by a committee since the heart of the book comes from many grandparents' favorite stories. Everyone jokes about the plethora of pictures grandparents pull out when any mention is made of grandchildren. However, since grandparenting is my business, I have heard many warm endearing anecdotes as well as sad and sometimes worrisome stories.

I may have lost some of the best stories. But as you read this book, look for yourself (even if not identified) in the universal, pervasive, all-inclusive thoughts and feelings that grandparents share.

So many of you have contributed to this book naming names is difficult for fear of leaving some of you out. First and foremost, I am indebted to Arthur and Carol Kornhaber whose pioneer research was the cornerstone for *The Joy of Grandparenting*; their encouragement continued as a lifeline. Many thanks to a kindred spirit, Marjorie Holmes, for her inspiration and motivation and to Tom and Nancy Osborne for their generous interest. My love and deepest thanks to my coffeepot friend and heart sister, Chrys Daniel, for listening, sharing and gently editing the manuscript.

Thank you to Ruby Gingles and Sally Van Zandt who fanned the spark of grandparenting in gerontology classes and I'm grateful to my personal "Board of Directors" — Elinor Caves, Sylvia Chalupsky, Marge Jessee, Terese Lux, Susan Macy, Jackie Robertson and Betty Stewart — who supported me before the book began.

Cooperative Extension Clubs and PEO Chapters were major contributors to the survey for my master's thesis. Thanks to SAGE Writers: Louis and Elizabeth Lindahl, Gordon and Sid Hahn Culver, Louella Corliss Spahn, Anne Johnson and others who listened and reviewed many of the chapters while writing memories for their grandchildren.

I appreciate those who shared books and newspaper clippings. Thank you to all the folks whose stories I've included without verifying the details. Many thanks to my Rosenquist, Carlson and Orr kinfolk for their support. Most of all I want to express my love and thanks to my children, their spouses and my grandchildren for their affection and patience during this late-life adventure.

And a heart full of appreciation to Linda Dageforde, my editor and publisher who kept telling me that we could do this...and has become a good friend.

A Taste of the Joy

Grandparenting has been my passion for the last twenty-five years. There was something about that little red-haired first grandbaby with flashing brown-eyes that changed my whole focus in life.

Most of what I know about grandparenting I learned from my parents and parents-in-law as they grandparented our four children. My parents and my husband's parents lived on farms only a few miles apart, a blessing in many ways. The support of all the grandparents made a difference for our young family— even though we look back on the '50s and '60s as innocent simpler times.

When our new babies arrived, our mothers cooperatively decided how they could help. When we took our little ones home for Christmas or vacations we usually spent the holidays with all grandparents. Our mothers talked on the telephone about their mutual grandchildren and became fast friends. It is still a comfort for me to envision Grandma Carlson and Grandma Orr sitting on a cloud chatting over the doings of their grandchildren — and now their great-grandchildren.

When I became a grandmother, long-distance grandparenting was my biggest challenge since my son, my grandson's father, was in the Air Force. This child of my child scampered in and out of my heart as he moved with his family around the country those first years. I checked the library for more information about grandparenting to no avail. Nostalgic poems and stories about grandmothers and cookie jars, attics and rocking chairs added to the classics of Little Red Riding Hood visiting her grandmother and Heidi's beloved grandfather. Twenty-five years ago grandparents had no real place or value in the family. In fact grandmothers were often considered meddlers. Social scientists wrote that "grandparenthood doesn't appear to be a high-impact life event." Fortunately, those thoughts do not prevail now.

I searched for ways to let my grandson, and later his two little brothers, know there was a grandma in Nebraska who cared about them. Knowing how much kids love to get letters, I used scraps of children's gift wrap to write simple love notes with lots of Xs and ❤s and adopted a round, happy face with glasses and a fuzzy hairdo as my signature. Reading books onto cassette tapes and sending the book and the tape to the boys worked well. The kids liked the rebate checks and toys sent directly to them after my film purchases. It was a game for me to find appropriate gifts not in the toy stores: a large boxful of all kinds of hats, an assortment of drawing utensils and paper for the budding artist, and small-size garden tools.

At this time I realized there were premarital classes, Lamaze classes, classes for new mothers and fathers, and classes for parents of adolescents, but there were no materials and no classes for grandparents. So, I shared grandparenting tips in workshops with women's groups and community college classes. People came "out of the closets" to learn more about grandparenting and talk about their grandchildren.

Wanting to learn more about the grandparent/grandchild relationship I went back to school while continuing to work at the University of Nebraska. Completing class work and a thesis based on a survey of 270 grandparents, I received a master's degree in time for the arrival of Alex, number ten grandchild.

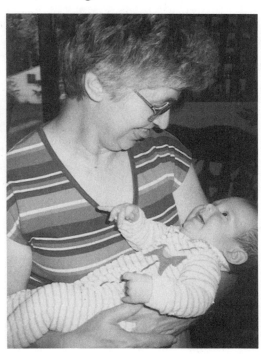

Alex, number ten grandchild, arrived in time to help celebrate Clarice's master's in Grandparenting.

Dr. Arthur Kornhaber and his wife Carol and their pioneer grandparenting study came to my attention through the book, *Grandparents/Grandchildren: The Vital Connection* co-authored with Kenneth L. Woodward. A pediatrician and child psychiatrist, Dr. Kornhaber discovered that when grandparents were included in children's psychiatric therapy, no matter how troubled the children were, the grandparents continued to "wax eloquent" about them. Kornhaber found that children have a magnetic attraction toward their grandparents and want to be on their good behavior, especially when with them. Troubled kids don't mind conflicts with their parents, but they don't want to embarrass or disappoint their grandparents. The Kornhabers' 1981 report identified five roles of grandparenthood that provide the "vital connection" between grandparents and grandchildren: historian, mentor, role model, wizard, and nurturer. Much of this theoretical work was included in his classes.

The Joy of Grandparenting book has evolved from 1) the early workshops sharing tips for keeping in touch, 2) my research survey, 3) the thesis for my master's degree, *The Grandparent/Grandchild Relationship: The Grandparents' Perspective*, 4) my color-slide-talk borrowed from family albums depicting grandparents' roles, 5) scores of conversations with grandparents and grandchildren, and 6) my best laboratory experience with my own ten grandchildren, five step-grandchildren and great-grands.

Although I've been promising to write *The Joy of Grandparenting* for many years, I actually contracted for the book on my birthday, December 28. I started writing on January 1, anticipating publication in nine months on September 1. Along about March I realized that I had eaten two big jars of dill pickles all by myself! It occurred to me that the book was growing inside of me and *The Joy of Grandparenting* was indeed my late-life baby.

The over-the-coffee cup conversations with other grandparents give this book authenticity and make the ideas workable in your own life. My neighbor Jackie reminds me of the importance of listening and talking to our peers — people at our same stage in life. She calls it "being with someone my own size." We remember how it was when we were raising our own children. After we shared our struggles of potty training or bad report cards with a friend or neighbor, we were better able to meet the problems of the day.

Life is the same now. Sometimes when she's in the middle of grandchildren's "busyness," Jackie comforts herself with the thought that she will soon be home and be with "someone my own size." I hope you will find that comfort in reading *The Joy of Grandparenting*.

People are hungry to learn about healthy, happy families. Grandparents are concerned about their children, grandchildren, and great-grandchildren. The day I signed on the dotted line for the publication of this book, I received a phone call from a woman I had never met. The soft voice on the other end of the line said, "I need help. When are you teaching classes on grandparenting? My grandson has just moved back to our town with my ex-daughter-in-law and there's a lot I don't know."

I hope this book conveys to the middle generation that grandparents are an extraordinary and powerful resource who can help them raise their children, and that young parents realize they hold the key to building this vital connection.

The job description for grandparents includes many tasks and responsibilities. We cannot all be Super-Grandparents and be all things to all grandchildren, but we take on different roles and obligations at different times. There's no right way to grandparent, but we are at our best when we build on our strengths and emphasize the positive aspects of our own extended family life.

When there are severe emotional problems as when we have physical health problems, it is a measure of strength to seek professional help and bring the family back to wholeness. Although you will find some discussion of problems in the chapter "Grandparents Are Security Blankets," this book focuses on wholeness and wellness.

My purpose is to inform grandparents, parents, and grandchildren of the value of the grandparent/grandchild relationship — the worth of the extended family. We touch the lives of our grandchildren in many ways, always having an influence whether for good or not. Grandchildren of all ages must also understand they add value and enrich the lives of their grandparents and great-grandparents.

It is important that all generations know that **GRANDPARENTS MAKE A DIFFERENCE.**

What Are Grandparents?

A grandma is to patch and mend,
To gather up the raveled ends,
To sew together tattered seams,
And iron out our wrinkled dreams.
— Clarice Orr

When our grandchild first utters any sound that is directed to us personally, a shiver of delight runs through our bones. Whatever name our little Dear One calls us we love it. Gramma, Grandma, Grandmother, Nana, MeeMaw, Granny, Gran, Grams — I've been called most of them. When you become a great-grandmother you can be G.G. One grandchild always called his grandmother "Sweetie;" I like that. Grandmothers in other lands are Bubbe, Obasan, Grossmuter, Nonna, Zumu, Babushka, Yia-Yia, Abuela and Ne-Neh. Swedish children learn different names for their mother's mother and father's mother—Mormor is the maternal grandmother and Farmor is the paternal grandmother.

Then there's Grampa, Grandpa, Grandfather, Bumpa, Poppa, Pop-Pop, Gramps — grandfathers will answer to any of them. In other countries grandfathers are called Deduskha, Ojisan, Zufu, Zaide, Grossvater, Grandpere, Kah-Keh, Nonno, Papou. In Sweden your father's father is Farfar and your mother's father is Morfar.

Hundreds of little books are available in gift and card shops extolling the feelings of awe and rapture that thoughts of grandma and grandpa bring to mind. Most everyone has something to say about grandparents. It might be that although we are not all grandparents, we all are grandchildren so that makes us all experts on the subject.

Charlie Shedd's book, *Then God Created Grandparents and It Was Very Good,* was one of the first grandparenting books I found and it is still a treasury of wit and wisdom. His answers to "What are grandparents for?" are the best.

- ❤ Grandparents are for wondering with you.
- ❤ Grandparents are for listening.
- ❤ Grandparents are for saying "no" sometimes.
- ❤ Grandparents are for having fun with you.
- ❤ Grandparents are for telling you what it used to be like, but not too much.
- ❤ Grandparents are for saying, "I think you're OK."

Patsy Gray was eight years old when she wrote the classic about grandmothers that was originally published in *PTA Magazine.* She wrote:

"A grandmother is a lady who has no children of her own so she likes other people's little boys and girls. A grandfather is a man grandmother...Grandmas don't have to do anything except be there. They are old, so they shouldn't play hard or run...Usually they are fat, but not too fat to tie the kids' shoes. They wear glasses, and they can take their teeth and gums off...They don't have to be smart, only answer questions like why dogs chase cats or how come God isn't married...When they read to us they don't skip words or mind if it is the same story again. Everybody should try to have one...because grandmas are the only grown-ups who have got time."

In 1988, Hallmark Cards, Inc. made a coffee mug that has always delighted me. At the top are the words, "Grandma always says..." and the sayings that follow seem to fit me to a tee:

- I don't know any kids who'd want these fresh cookies, do you?
- Come give Grandma a B-I-I-G kiss.
- What's the magic word?
- You wear me out just watchin' you.
- We'll buy it and if your Mom won't let you have it, you can play with it at MY house.
- I just might have an extra quarter in my purse.
- No fourths? You don't like my cooking?
- Are you SURE your mother lets you do this?
- We've got to fatten you up.
- Sit right here on my lap and I'll read you a story.
- That's what grandmas are for.
- Grandma loves you too!

Sometime ago, Erma Bombeck wrote a job description for grandparents. She said something like:

"A grandmother will put a sweater on you when she is cold, feed you when she is hungry, and send you to bed when she is tired...A

grandmother can be counted on to buy anything from all-purpose greeting cards to ten
chances on a pony...And a grandparent will
pretend he doesn't know you on Halloween."

I didn't have to fill out a job application when I first
became a grandmother. In fact, no one even asked me if
I wanted the job. I'm not sure I would have accepted if
I'd know the job specifications. However, after twenty
years of experience, with ten grandchildren, two step-
grandchildren and three step-great-grandchildren, (you
know what the next line is) I wouldn't give up my job
for a million dollars.

This has gotten me to thinking about what it takes
to be a grandmother. If I were to begin a Rent-a-Grand-
mother service, this is the way my job description would
look in the want ad section of the newspaper.

Be-a-Grandmother

Lifetime position with responsibility for the happiness, growth and
development of grandchildren
from birth on beyond maturity.
Work under supervision of directors of progressive family-oriented
organization anticipating expan-
sion. Hours varied. Not an 8-5 job.
May work out of own home. May
be some travel.

Higher education not required,
but previous experience as pediatrician or psychiatrist helpful. Must
have extensive knowledge of human relations. Computer experience not necessary—in five or six
years, grandchild will train. Skill in
reading aloud essential.

Successful applicant will have
multiple duties and functions: magician, cheerleader, playmate,
kinkeeper, bridgebuilder, hero, beacon, security blanket and sage.

Individual must be loving, self-
motivated, loving, caring, loving,
selfless, loving, accepting, loving
and loving.

Salary: Seven figures—
$0,000,000 annually. Fringe benefits
include some meals and occasional
overnight accommodations in addition to generous hugs and kisses, at
first wet and sticky.

Write to P.O. Box 1000, Any-
where, USA listing availability. Request additional information regarding specific tasks and tools required. All inquiries are publicized
immediately. Be-a-Grandmother is
an Equal Opportunity/Affirmative
Action employer, except interested
males please see Be-a-Grandfather
listing.

Mrs. MacFarlane, a pioneer farm woman who helped my grandmother at the birth of my father in 1898, gave this poem to me when she was 94 years old and I became a grandmother. She never had any children or grandchildren and I marvel at her interest in clipping and saving this anonymous poem for me.

The old rocking chair is vacant today
For Grandma is no longer in it.
She's off in her car to her office or shop:
Just buzzing around every minute.
No one shoves Grandma back on the shelf,
She is versatile, forceful, dynamic —
That isn't a pie in the oven, my dear
Her baking today is ceramic!
You won't see her trundle off early to bed
Or seek out a warm comfy nook;
Her typewriter clackety-clacks half the night —
For Grandma is writing a book.
Without ever taking a look at past years
To slow down her steady advancing
She won't tend the babies for you anymore —
For Grandma has taken up dancing!
She isn't content with the crumbs of Old Thoughts,
With meager or second-hand knowledge;
Don't bring your mending for Grandma to do —
For Grandma has gone back to college!

♥x♥x♥x♥x♥x♥x♥x♥x♥

Grandparents Make A Difference

*What children are looking for is a hug, a lap,
a kind word, a touch, someone to read them
a story, somebody to smile and share with.*
— John Thompson

All grandparents like to talk about their grandchildren — that's a fact, no one disputes that thought. Everyone likes to talk about their grandparents. Part of the charm and delight in reminiscing is considering how our grandparents were different than we are as grandparents.

Grandparents come in all styles, shapes, colors and sizes. An enchanting children's book, *Our Granny*, with the story by Margaret Wild has delightful pictures by Julie Vivas illustrating that some grannies have thin legs, fat knees, bristly chins, interesting hair, crinkly eyes, big soft laps and wobbly bottoms.

Recently, Grandma Demerath and I were remembering that Little John called me his "Reading Grandma" and she was his "Cookie Grandma." We agreed that we have changed almost as much as he has in twenty-five years. She seldom bakes cookies and I *listen* to books while I'm driving. Times have changed. Priorities change and technology allows us to make changes easily.

All four of my grandparents were pioneers on the prairies of South Dakota in the 1880s. I'm sort of a pioneer, too. I was born on the Carlson homestead and went to country school through the eighth grade, always the only student in my grade with six to eight other pupils. As a junior in high school, I attended a regional meeting in Beaver Dam, Wisconsin, with a dozen girls and a few educators, when our purpose was to write the constitution for the young Future Homemakers of America.

After high school graduation, I went to Dakota Wesleyan University and attended an experimental class on marriage taught by the school nurse. We met in the chemistry lab in the basement of Science Hall at 4:30 on Monday afternoons. I believed in the concept of education for marriage so I wrote an oration cleverly titled (I thought) "The MRS Degree."

After that class, I thought I knew everything so John and I were married and had four children in the next five years. Fifteen years later after typing for my husband's doctoral dissertation I went back to college, joining another pioneer class studying the middle years of human development. I experienced typical middlescence — evaluating where I was and what I wanted to do with the rest of my life. I continued to work at the University of Nebraska and finished my bachelor's degree graduating with my oldest daughter. And in the meantime I became a grandmother!

This was my second chance. I was a young grandmother and with most of my children out of the nest, I could be what I think I always wanted to be — a grandmother. Someone who could enjoy the little kids and not be responsible for them — someone who could read story books, play games, crochet afghans and knit cute little sweaters. And not have to worry about diapers and bottles, buying shoes and school supplies. When you become a grandparent you realize that things are different than when you were a kid.

In my life there's a strong sense of family although I did not have a close relationship with my grandparents. Grandma and Grandpa Carlson moved to town when my parents married and took over the farm. By the time I was six years old, both paternal grandparents had died. Growing up in the house that Grandpa and Grandma Carlson had built before South Dakota was a state, helped me get to know them. I snooped in the closets and drawers of the old house, rummaged through vintage apparel, tried on old-fashioned shoes and hats and found underclothes unknown to me. The by-gone sepia faces of "shirt-tail" relatives in photos and snapshots are etched in my memory.

Communication with my grandparents was limited since none of them learned English until they came to America as young adults. "Us kids" learned only a few words of Swedish. We could say *tak sa mycket* — thank you — when we left Grandma and Grandpa's and we knew *pojka* meant boy and *flicka* meant girl. My maternal grandparents were a part of my life longer so I knew them better, however, Grandma Rosenquist's profound deafness created another communication barrier.

After we finished our "trading"— sold the eggs and cream and bought the groceries for the next week — we stopped at Grandma and Grandpa Rosenquist's in town on late Saturday afternoons. I remember sitting around Grandma's dining room table and dunking her sweet molasses-flavored rye bread into my coffee diluted with cream. Later, while Mom and Grandma talked over the events, I sneaked up to the attic. In the corner was the spinning wheel that Grandma brought along on the boat. Now that spinning wheel is nestled in the corner of my own living room. Grandpa always sat in a captain's chair by the radio. He teased us kids, trying to catch an arm or leg with his cane as we slipped by.

We were not a picture-perfect family. My grandparents faced many of the same problems we know today. Grandparents raised grandchildren. There was family abuse, divorce, abandonment, depression and alcoholism. Our family had Downs Syndrome children. Grandbabies died. Uncle Eskel died as a young father and Aunt Elna died of cancer leaving three youngsters. Aunt Minnie, who raised her own five as a single parent, mothered her sister's little ones with help from cousins, aunts and uncles. My father didn't know that farm living prolonged his battle with asthma and emphysema until it was almost too late. Now, these recollections remind me of my tough family heritage. My grandparents continue to have an influence on my life even in my later years.

My children's grandparents made a difference in my life and touched my children's lives in many ways. Now we grandparents wonder if and how we can have an influence or make a difference in the lives of our grandchildren. That's the purpose of this book — to tell you that you are important in the life of your grandchildren — that you can make a difference.

Grandparents make a difference in all the different roles we play — Magicians, Cheerleaders, Playmates, Kinkeepers, Bridgebuilders, Heroes, Beacons, Security Blankets and Sages. In the following pages each role is studied more critically, but this chapter gives a taste of the Joy of Grandparenting as I sense my grandparents and my children's grandparents made a difference.

When my children talk about their Grandpa Carlson, someone usually remembers that he always carried several rolls of candy Lifesavers in his pocket and they got to choose their favorite flavor. But what made them really proud was when visiting Grandpa's church on Sunday mornings, their Grandpa became the Candy Man. After the last "Amen" all the little kids would find my dad and he would patiently dole out Lifesavers, "sprinkling stardust in their eyes" almost as if he were a MAGICIAN.

Grandpa Rosenquist gave me candy, too — little chalky-white peppermint buttons and bright pink wintergreen-flavored mints. I didn't care for the candy so much but always accepted it because I knew it pleased him to give me a little treat once in awhile. (Are grandchildren like that now? Do you suppose my grandchildren accept some of my gifts because they don't want to hurt my feelings?)

As CHEERLEADERS, grandparents show their explicit faith in their grandchildren. My mother told the story that when Grandpa August Carlson saw my brother Loren as a newborn, he prophesied, "That boy will be governor some day." Loren did not become governor of our state but he has had a lifetime interest in politics and continues to teach political science at the University of South Dakota. How much Grandpa Carlson's remark influenced Loren's political career is hard to know.

I don't remember my grandparents as PLAYMATES. They were old! However Grandpa would tease us and tell us stories and we had fun when we went to their house. They didn't approve of cards and the only game I remember was a carom board. Grandpa kept a child's wagon in the garage and we thought it was great sport pulling each other up and down the sidewalk since there wasn't much concrete on the farm.

My children's Grandpa Orr loved to take the children fishing. To him, this was fun and relaxation. He made it a big expedition — the planning was the biggest part of the fun. He would talk about it for weeks ahead of time. Grandma Orr would fix an elegant picnic with fried chicken, potato salad, Jello and most important — a big watermelon. Cutting and eating the watermelon was a ritual that Grandpa captured on his 8 mm movie camera. Later when we went back to visit, we enjoyed the watermelon all over again as we watched the movies.

Grandma and Grandpa Orr worked hard to be playmates with their grandchildren. Before we had a swing set in our backyard, Grandpa Orr put one up when the family was home for their fortieth anniversary. When we were all together on the farm one Fourth of July, Grandpa purchased a magnificent set of fireworks.

All my grandparents were family historians and KINKEEPERS. They fostered a sense of kinship and family for us. I was number 24 grandchild of 32 Carlson cousins, all who lived within ten miles of us. On the Rosenquist side, I was number eight of thirteen cousins, who, with three pairs of aunts and uncles, lived in other parts of the country. Considering this conglomeration of kinfolk, it's hard to think that my arrival had much impact outside my parents' house.

However, my birth on Sunday, December 28, 1930, following the traditional Carlson family Christmas dinner, imprinted the "family feeling" on my identity. I thought it was my "bad luck" to get presents for a "Merry Christmas and a Happy Birthday." The truth is that the Carlsons continued to get together each Christmas and my birthdate was acknowledged if not celebrated each year. Perhaps that bit of recognition by my extended family gave me a special niche.

At times I felt as if I grew up an only child although I had four brothers and Cousin Jim lived with us. Now, it seems being born female and weighing five pounds made a difference. It also made a difference that I was born at the height of the Great Depression and Dust

Bowl Era during a South Dakota winter, two years after the death of my brother Dennis, who had lived only a year. My folks sheltered and babied me until my brother Keith's arrival three-and-a-half years later diminished my princess status. I was blessed with many who cared for me although I was unaware of their loving concern until a later time when strong support from my cousins meant a lot.

Grandma and Grandpa Carlson were BRIDGE-BUILDERS. The stories of these caring and courageous pioneer ancestors are retold by their great-grandchildren. They each had only a few years of schooling in Sweden, learning to speak and read English after they came to the United States as young adults. Grandpa didn't write English very well but with the help of a public stenographer he submitted many letters to the editor on topics concerning the welfare of his fellow farmers. All my grandparents were active in building churches and schools that made our community a better place. They all assumed their responsibilities as good citizens.

Grandma and Grandpa Carlson went to court and became the legal guardians for their first grandson Jim. Jim's father, their son Eskel, had died after Jim's mother had left them. Although she came back to get her son, Jim chose to live with my grandparents and the judge awarded them custody. My grandparents accepted this commitment much as grandparents who raise their grandchildren these days.

All my grandparents were HEROES as they overcame the hardships as new immigrants and battled the blizzards, drought, prairie fires and unfamiliar farming conditions. They persisted against adversity and demonstrated the virtues of good character. To me they were living examples of courage and faith. I remember a story about Grandpa Rosenquist. That Sunday his wheat was

THE FAMILY CIRCUS **By Bil Keane**

2-7
Copyright 1985
The Register and Tribune
Syndicate, Inc.

"Well, yes — we'll see Granddad someday when we go to heaven."

"Could I just wait in the car?"

REPRINTED WITH PERMISSION OF BIL KEANE, GRANDFATHER OF 8.

ripe for harvest, but Grandpa took his family to church while his neighbor cut his own grain. A storm destroyed Grandpa's field that year, but the next year the hail stopped at the road and his corn was a bumper crop.

My daughters Cheryle and Cyndi remember my parents as BEACONS whose spiritual values still touch them. Each daughter related the same memory of Grandma and Grandpa Carlson to me at different times. They told of their pleasant, gentle feelings of waking up at Grandma and Grandpa's and finding them at the kitchen table with the toaster and Bible between them.

Each morning Grandma read a portion of the Bible and an inspirational meditation. This spiritual sense between my children and their grandparents has been lasting and meaningful.

To think of grandparents as SECURITY BLANKETS I hope to convey the thought that grandparents provide a safe place for us, a shelter, a haven, a sanctuary. This chapter considers problems that grandparents face in our society. Most of us deal with divorce and/or blended families with step-grandchildren. We find special challenges with grandchildren who are chronically or terminally ill. We face problems of emotionally handicapped grandkids and even gifted children cause stress. When our adult children have miscarriages, abortions or cannot have children, we grieve. When we get a terrible phone call of a bad accident, we want to be there to comfort whoever needs it the most. Grandparents as the emotional heads of the extended family have a big job to be that safe shelter.

We often think of grandparents as SAGES, the wise elders. Most of us recall some pithy proverb that a grandparent "always" said that seemed to fit all occasions. These sayings range from "Too many cooks spoil the broth" and "Never let the sun go down on your wrath" to "Always wear clean underwear" and "Do unto others as you would have them do unto you."

In this chapter about wise grandparents, you will read about ordinary grandparents who do extra-ordinary things outside their family circles. Grandmother Waunda raised her own granddaughter and continues as the unofficial "church grandmother." Tom and Nancy Osborne have unofficially "raised" many Cornhusker football players and also cherish their role as grandparents to William.

The theme of this book is that *Grandparents Make a Difference* in the lives of their grandchildren. The last chapter recognizes that **GrandCHILDREN Make a Difference.** Grandparents are healthier and happier because of their grandchildren. Grandchildren make us laugh and they make us proud. They keep us young, energize us and empower us. They give us an excuse to shop. Because of our grandchildren we remember when we were kids and they remind us to be nice to others. Grandchildren keep us out of the ruts of life and they keep us honest. Most important, grandchildren give purpose and appreciation for our lives since grandchildren are our promise for the future.

As you read the ideas and suggestions in *The Joy of Grandparenting*, I hope to affirm your value as grandparents, grandchildren and parents in the grandparent/grandchild relationship. I encourage you to seek new opportunities to make a difference.

Grandma Esther learned about opportunity from her grandson. Two-year-old Matthew sometimes uses his sturdy build to take advantage of his five-year-old sister Emily. In a squabble, Matthew grabbed a toy from Emily. But when he dropped it, she quickly recovered it. Matthew went crying to his mother wanting to regain possession of the pilfered plaything. Mother explained that when Matthew dropped the toy, Emily had seized the opportunity to retrieve it and the toy was now rightfully hers. Matthew was not to be dissuaded and loudly protested, "It's MY OPPORTUNITY!"

Dear readers, I hope, like little Matthew, you insist that now is your opportunity to learn more of *The Joy of Grandparenting* and your families will realize, that indeed, **Grandparents Make a Difference.**

Grandparents Are Magicians

Grandparents can do more
for us than anyone else in the world;
they sprinkle stardust in our eyes.
— Alex Haley, author of *Roots*

randparents are MAGICIANS when they create something wonderful out of nothing or some bit of magic produces a surprise of joy and happiness with very little effort. Love alone accomplishes mini miracles. We grandparents are magicians or wizards when we engage in fanciful, pleasurable activity to the pure delight of our grandchildren. When we make it happen for our grandkids some of the magic potion rubs off on us and we know that same joy.

Grandparents can make marvels out of the ordinary things of life. You know, some of us can take out our teeth or unplug our ears. Grandparents can bake, from scratch, cinnamon rolls that linger in our taste buds forever. I am still looking for the Swedish rye bread that tastes like Grandma Rosenquist's. Nothing ever measures up. Recently, telling my brother Loren about my search for Grandma's rye bread, I learned he saw things in a different light. "I never liked Grandma's bread. It was too heavy," he said.

Thinking of grandparents as magicians, Dr. Harold Edgerton, the real-life wizard, who "bottled lightning" when he invented the strobe light and the electronic camera flash comes to mind. It was my joy to know this enchanting, kind, humble gentleman. He not only performed magic for the world with his inventions, but he was a Super-Grandfather, too. He took his grandchildren along on undersea explorations he made with Jacques Cousteau on the ship, *Calypso*. He took them one-at-a-time preferring to take them at the "perfect" age of 11. "Then you can still boss 'em," he told me. Can you imagine how little Ellen felt going along on the expedition to Scotland when Grandpa Edgerton searched for the Loch Ness Monster? "She was my go-fer," he confided. "She'd go-fer this and go-fer that, for me."

When I asked Grandmother Esther Edgerton what grandparents could do for their grandchildren, her answer was brief but not simple, "We can give them roots and wings." While they were able, the Edgertons came back from Boston frequently to revisit their roots in Nebraska. They erected markers in the town of Aurora and on Esther's family farm in memory of their pioneer parents. Doc Edgerton said, "We have to help history along a little." Knowing their roots, grandchildren have the stability and fundamentals to give wings to their visions and dreams.

A few years ago, *USA Today* asked readers to write about being a grandparent. Frank Cooper, of Everett, Washington, wrote of a day he spent with three grandchildren helping them build a dog house. He promised a wiener roast when the project was completed. However, Grandpa had forgotten the "potential mayhem of the paint mess, kids, brushes and carport," and suggested that Grandmother heat the wieners on the stove.

Cooper realized he was "trying to weasel out of his promise," so he reluctantly built a fire in the backyard fire-pit and the wieners were properly roasted and devoured. As they relaxed and watched the embers die down, six-year-old Jeffrey leaned against his grandfather's chest and made all the effort worthwhile. "Know what, Grampa?" he asked. "This is the best day of my whole life."

For long-distance grandchildren, visits from grandparents are often heralded like a holiday. Parents build up our pending arrival with anticipation of wonderful things happening: "We'll get a puppy when Grandma comes," or "Maybe Grandpa will take you to the zoo when he comes."

My dentist told me his plans to put together a fancy swing set for his granddaughter who lives in another city. The three-year-old pestered "Poppa" with phone calls asking when he was going to build her playground equipment. He told her he would get to it in June. "Oh," she said and turning from the phone she asked her mother, "When's June?" In another phone call the little one promised she and her mother "will make some shookies. And when you're all done, Poppa, we'll go up in the treehouse and eat shookies." That was an offer Grandfather could not resist; the building project began the next weekend.

A pair of South Dakota grandparents created some magic early one winter. Grandpa Ray and Grandma Loretta planned to visit their grandson who lived a couple hundred miles south of them for Thanksgiving. The grandparents' area had a major snowstorm although the roads were cleared. This enterprising pair took a do-it-yourself snowman along in the trunk of their car. What fun they had secretly setting up the snowman outside their grandson's window. Can you imagine how special that little boy felt to have the only snowman in town?

How do you transport a snowman? It isn't too tough. You roll some big snowballs and put them each in a big leaf bag or garbage bag. Take along an old hat, a scarf and a carrot for a nose and you have an easy-to-assemble snowman.

One year our family had a magical holiday retreat at Vacation Village in San Diego. Half of our family lived in California and the rest of us flew in. Planning this wondrous Christmas had begun a whole year before. We went to the famed San Diego Zoo and made all the tourist stops. But Carrie, who was four, was enraptured that our beach houses faced directly on the bay. She let me think that we had created this magical time for her. She said, "I've never had my very own ocean before."

While at my brother Paul's funeral in Maryland, I learned that he truly was a magician. He went to classes to learn prestidigitation and sleight of hand tricks of amateur sorcerers. When their family gathered for annual get-togethers at the beach, Paul was always prepared to perform. Before the funeral, we noticed that the grandkids had plugged in a video of one of his performances. On the screen his grandkids jumped up and down volunteering to be the magician's helper. Chrissa struggled with the scissors to cut the clothes line rope in two and she gasped in wonderment when Paul produced it whole again.

We were mystified with his card tricks and disappearing and reappearing coins. We cried and we laughed and we cried some more. My sister-in-law — the grandkids call her MeeMaw — brought out the magic box that Paul had created with his pseudonym on the top, The Great Ellsworth. From the box, the grandchildren each chose their favorite trick to take home with them. Kevin, the oldest grandson, got to keep the magic box. Through the wizardry of video I saw my brother alive again as The Great Ellsworth. Like his grandkids, I knew that same feeling that Paul had made something miraculous happen.

Not an amateur magician like my brother Paul, I have one little trick that always delights my grandchildren — making bubbles. And again, it doesn't cost much but a little preparation.

♥x♥x♥x♥x♥x♥x♥x♥x♥

Grandma Orr's Giant Bubbles

1 gallon of water
1 cup of Dawn
   or Joy liquid detergent
1/3 to 1/2 cup
   of white Karo syrup

♥x♥x♥x♥x♥x♥x♥x♥x♥

That's all there is to making giant bubbles. For a bubble machine, draw a length of yarn through two soda straws and tie together to make a box shape. Cut the center out of a plastic foam plate and the rim becomes a bubble machine. Or bend a wire coathanger into a ring and cover the sharp ends with a piece of electrical or

Carrie, 12, made the very best bubble ever!

plastic tape. Pour bubble liquid into a plastic dishpan or metal cakepan. Warm humid days with no wind are the best bubble days. Store bubble solution in empty detergent bottles; it gets better with age. If you are really adventurous, make up 5 gallons of solution and pour it in a child's wading pool. Use a hula hoop to make huge tunnels of bubbles. Have the child stand on a stool or box in the wading pool and enclose the child in a bubble! Bubbles are fun for everyone from 1 to 100. My friends of all ages know they may be making bubbles when they are invited to my house!

Grandparents are a little like the Easter Bunny and Santa Claus. Ol' Saint Nick must be the patron saint of grandparents. What other times of year (besides Valentine's Day, birthdays, May Day, or Halloween — it sorta adds up!) do we allow ourselves to indulge in the over-generosities of the pocketbook? Grandmother/writer Lois Wyse says she qualifies to be called "Shop-Along-Cassidy." We search out every WalMart and Toys 'R' Us to find the special gift we know will enthrall our grandchild forever. But, perhaps we realize there are other issues at hand. Are we trying to buy our grandchild's love and affection? Does the gift please the parents (even if it's not a noisy drum)? Are we concerned what the other grandparents give for gifts?

Finding a unique gift for a special child is difficult. Elders want to give something that will have lasting value for the child and not just another battery operated toy that seems to be the most popular toy this year. My grandchildren's parents often give the "TV gift-of-the-year" to make sure their children are not disappointed. Some of those gifts are too expensive for me and I have to figure out something else.

A dear friend, Grandmother Ruby G., told me long ago that the very best gift for a child, or anyone for that matter, is the Gift of Time. This gift may actually be time spent with the child. My California grandsons, Phillip and Michael, have birthdays near Thanksgiving and Christmas and since I seldom see them, coupons for

"Grandma Time" to be used at their discretion when I am visiting in their home seem to work.

On one visit, Phillip chose to use his "Grandma Time" to give me a tour of their acreage, their ball field and the garden. He helped me up and down the rocks as we tramped through the brush. A couple of deer scampered ahead of us and other little creatures wriggled through the tall, dry grass. Phillip showed me the fort he built from the construction leftovers. After the tour, he climbed some of the trees to knock down the delicate Spanish moss that draped the trees on the ridge. Another time, Michael used his Grandma Time Coupon at a small amusement center where he drove a gasoline-powered car. I think he also persuaded me to watch him hit golf balls.

The gift of time might also be used in writing a letter, baking cookies, searching for a very special gift to purchase or for making crafts and handmade gifts.

A long time ago, my mother offered this gift-giving advice:

Give
  Something for the child's mind,
      ❤ a book or puzzle
  Something for the child's physical needs,
      ❤ clothing, scarves, mittens
  Something for fun
      ❤ a toy or game

Gift-giving is a major dilemma for many grandparents. Whether your son is vice-president of a major toy company or your daughter is a waitress at the local diner, you want to give something that is appropriate and unique for your special grandchild and also fits your pocketbook.

Grandmothers are known to anticipate blessed events as the time to get clacking on their knitting needles and crochet hooks making afghans, sweaters and booties. Most grandmas have stopped hemming flannel for diapers and sewing layettes as my mother did for my children.

The most beautiful handwork I have ever seen was the exquisite baby blue satin carriage robe tucked and smocked by my first-born's grandmother. It was so elegant I hardly dared use it, but was always proud to have it. That precious cover is now in my son's possession awaiting the arrival of his grandchild.

A lot of magic is created on sewing machines. Claire and Emilie still have the teddy bears dressed in wedding dresses that I made when they were little. Cousin Christina's grandson Ian asked for a Star Trek suit via their fax machines. (You wouldn't expect a Pony Express rider to deliver a request for a space age outfit like that!) With red and black spandex swimsuit material Christina designed and fashioned the apparel from the various fax illustrations Ian sent. She added a patch that "emanates from a laser and simulates the telecommand."

Handmade dolls, doll clothes, teddy bears and stuffed animals are right for kids of most ages. My daughters treasure the Raggedy Anns and Andys that my mother made for them as teens. Look in the needlework department and craft shops for specialty kits for that perfect gift. *Wizard of Oz* character dolls seemed right for my grandsons — the Tin Man, the Cowardly Lion and the Scarecrow. Teen-agers, even boys, like Nebraska's Herbie Husker or mascots of national sports teams. Use glue guns to make fancy apparel for inexpensive teddy bears or to create a fancy dress for a doll. Glue some angel wings or feathers on a small stuffed animal and add some old costume jewelry for your own creation.

Grandmothers use needles, thread and thimbles to make quilts and covers. Make blankets for dollies or "blankies" for toddlers. Grandma Chrys, who doesn't sew, discovered a ready-made quilted placemat was just right for Betsy's doll bed. My sister-in-law has made dozens of small patchwork quilts out of flannel pieces tied to a soft backing. My grandchildren loved Aunt Violet's cuddly quilts so much that their mother has also taken to making them. Their friends in Australia and Germany are pleased with these American-crafted patchwork baby gifts.

Bind a square of soft terry cloth making a hooded bath towel when you put a triangular piece of cloth in the corner. If the hood is decorated with the face of a teddy bear and ears are added, an infant can be wrapped in it as a Halloween costume. Since kids love pretending to be Superman, circus performers or magicians, an appropriate cape can be made by binding a single piece of satin or other glamorous fabric — either with needle and thread or with a glue gun. Caution must be used that the length of the cape doesn't cause the child to trip. The opening for the neckline or the fastening at the neck must not be restricted. Kids even make capes for themselves.

T-shirts and sweatshirts make great gifts for anyone anytime. Especially when you design it yourself or have it made. My niece, Kelley, has a business of making shirts for any occasion — she made shirts with watermelon slices for the Carlson Reunion. Kelley's shirts are works of art, she creates the designs, appliquéing and painting each shirt individually.

An old-time photo copied on a shirt is a fun gift. Find a picture of grandma's family and take it to the local T-shirt "factory" to be reproduced. You'll make a hit if you put a baby picture of your adult child on a nightshirt for a teen-age granddaughter.

Grandma Dorothy specializes in making porcelain dolls for her grandchildren. Nicole and Kaeleigh have received ballerinas, baby dolls and dolls dressed in First Communion dresses that duplicate the girls'. Dorothy creates the doll heads from the clay slip, putting the dolls together with body parts of porcelain, painting each delicate fingernail, dimple or tummy button or sometimes she carefully crafts cloth bodies. She fashions authentic, fabulous clothing for her creations, mostly from fabric salvaged from garage sales.

Last summer, Dorothy decided it was time to share her skills with her granddaughters. In a marathon of a few days' activity, Dorothy and her granddaughters each created a baby doll. Nicole and Kaeleigh poured the molds for the heads, fired them, painted the features and produced the cloth body form all by themselves. Two young girls have sweet memories of that special summer they learned how to make their own dolly.

Grandfathers are often wizards at woodworking. Grandpa Dick worked for weeks in his basement, gluing each tiny shingle and dado, before he proudly delivered the clapboard Victorian dollhouse to Adrienne. Grandfathers make heirloom cradles for their new grandbabes. Doll beds and child-size tables and chairs keep grandpas occupied in their workshops.

My son-in-law's Uncle Bill, who lives on "Golden Pond" in upstate New York, built two unique blocks or cubes for my granddaughter that can become whatever she imagines. Three identical wooden sides in a U-shape have a fourth side of the same size fit into the U equidistant between the top and the bottom to make a seat and give the U-shape solidity. One block can be used as a seat and another block can be turned over to become a table. The blocks can be lined up as a train or stacked on top of each other for toy shelves.

Uncle Bill's Play Boxes
or
Claire's Chairs

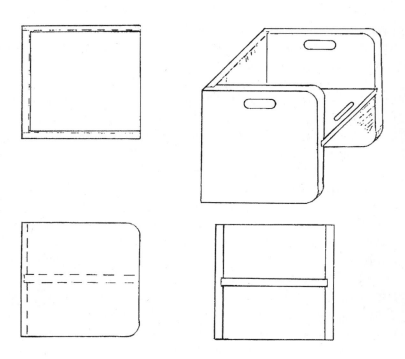

This all-purpose cube is a great idea for you toddler grandchild. It is a sturdy step stool. Or use two together as a chair and tip one over for a table. Line them up and play train. Stack them and they become toy shelves. Stacked in another direction two cubes become a night stand. Made of 3/4" plywood, keep in mind that each piece of the three sides is a square whether it is 12" or 15". The seat or crosspiece is midway. Round the corners. Make keyhole handles in the sides and seat. Paint or stain as you desire. Enjoy your grandchild having fun!

I matted and framed, inexpensively, some old Deanna Durbin paper dolls from my girlhood and passed them on to a granddaughter.

Sleeping bags and pillows made from drapery remnants make a hit with kids for TV watching. Bags to hold their paraphernalia and pillows are great to have in the family van. Denim works great; you can make tote bags from the bottoms of jeans' legs when the jeans become cutoffs. Since three grandsons' father was in the Air Force they traveled often and they liked having their own pillows wherever they were.

A small shelf for a grandchild's room is a good place to park collections and stuff. My friend Dorothy personalized Emilie's and Claire's shelves by painting their names and sweet flowers on them. A small reading lamp and a low bookcase that fits next to the child's bed encourages them to read or look at books. A pediatrician suggested that allowing children to turn out their lights, when they are ready, gives them control and responsibility for themselves. Having that responsibility empowers children and gives them self-confidence.

Self-recorded cassette tapes proved to be some of the kids' best gifts. Read a favorite book onto a tape and send the book and the tape to the child. The child learns to recognize your voice as you talk directly to him. It works well if you can have the child on your lap to record the story and then give the book and the tape to the child. Not only for grandchildren who live away from you, tapes are welcomed by their busy parents at naptime and/or when the children are in their car seats.

Of course, telling your own stories onto cassette tapes is even better and is good for any age. Tell your special children about their parents or grandparents in their growing up years...not just the hardships, but the times they — or you as a child — got into trouble and what happened.

Tape recorders make excellent gifts, standard models and child size models. Some children like to pretend they are TV stars and make and listen to their own recordings. When Phillip was about three he loved to pretend he was a master of ceremonies. At 15, he continues to have great stage presence as a symphony concert performer.

Museum catalogs — such as the catalog from the Massachusetts Institute of Technology Museum — contain wonderful ideas for T-shirts, brain-teasers, books, games and puzzles that you don't find at the mall. These gifts may challenge the youngster in educational ways that many toy manufacturers do not. You can find gift ideas for hard-to-buy-for young men in museums — particularly sons-in-law.

Magazine subscriptions are also suggested in the Bridgebuilders chapter. *National Geographic World* is good for elementary kids. And there is *Ranger Rick* by the National Wildlife Society, in addition to the *Sesame Street* and *Highlights* classics. My mother gave the *Reader's Digest* to my son when he was ten; it made him think he was grown up.

One Christmas I sent my grandsons a **box full of hats**. I found or made all kinds of hats — lady's, cowboy's, magician's, witch's, policeman's, railroad engineer's, chef's, a Native American feather headdress and a farmer's seed corn hat. The hats fit in a sturdy purchased storage box. You could easily make a similar dress-up box for little girls. Or keep dress-up clothes in a closet for the grandkids to play with when they come to visit. Old formals and long dresses, even old slips, nightgowns and aprons seem elegant to little girls. This is their costume resource for the plays they produce when they visit.

Some good sturdy small garden tools and small "glubs" were perfect for Phillip when he was about five and loved to work in the garden with his mother.

Grandkids who like to play office and business professional will appreciate a box of "office equipment" — little spiral notebooks, ballpoint and felt-tip pens, Scotch tape for their very own, child-safe scissors and a small stapler. Mark liked to draw and I sent him drawing equipment — colored paper, drawing tablets, colored pencils and small paperback books about cartooning and lettering.

Children love to receive as gifts those treats reserved for only special occasions. We have a photo of an ecstatic Claire, the Christmas she was three years old, holding a favorite gift that year — her very own litre of Pepsi. A friend's grandson was crazy over his very own Tombstone pizza.

I like to write special letters for particular birthdays — such as the 10th, 16th, 21st. Tell the grandchildren your memories of the day they were born...what was happening in your life, how you felt when you heard the news. Or what you remember about being 10 or 16 or 21. Select age-appropriate stationery and use your own best handwriting. This letter may become a cherished keepsake that will be handed down to their children. **Write a poem and frame it**, with each line beginning with a letter in the child's name. For example:

Michael, 10, demonstrates the discipline demanded by karate.

M ichael is great at karate.
I   t keeps him sharp and fit.
C hoosing to practice often,
H e doesn't argue a bit.
A nd he's quite a golfer.
E ven when it rains.
L et's all cheer for Michael!

P raise him until he complains.

It's not great poetry but maybe Michael will like it. I'm sure you can do better for your grandchild.

Write a story about your grandchild and his or her favorite toy. When John III was small, I wrote about "Johnny and the Magic Helmet"— a very simple story about him and his daddy's Air Force helmet. The pages were stapled together with spaces for Johnny to illustrate his own book.

Write your own story for your grandchild — telling your memories of Christmas and birthday celebrations. Write about baking your first cake or pie. About the trips you took, the school you went to, the cars your parents had. About the dogs and cats you had, the chores you did. You may have been given a special "fill-in-the-blank" book for grandparents available in many bookstores. You might also find an "empty" book that is just right for your very own story.

Pretty cloth covered books also can be given as gifts for diaries, journals or travel books. Or maybe you want to jot down some of your favorite recipes in one of those charming empty books for a grandchild. Note where you got the recipe and when you use it. A young person would treasure your own collection of favorite sayings — this could be your very own personalized "Instruction Book for Living."

With a big family to remember at Christmas, it's sometimes overwhelming to decide what to give as gifts. **Help yourself by giving the same gift to everyone.** Then you don't have to decide what to give. For example, give gloves and mittens to everyone. Or T-shirts. Or books. Or plan to give the same gift to each grandchild at a certain age — a *Bible* when they are twelve, or a *Webster's Dictionary* when they are fifteen. Children love tradition and rituals, it gives them something to look forward to. They want to be treated equally — as equally as you can! Remember that fair and equal is not always the same.

Grandfather Ed and Grandmother Marguerite have nineteen grandchildren. Many years ago they wisely decided to give savings bonds as birthday gifts. Their oldest grandson used some of his bonds during college and other children are appreciating the extra funds that have been earning interest through the years. Meanwhile, Ed and Marguerite's bond purchases continue as long as new grandchildren keep arriving.

Gladys B., my mother's childhood friend, is ninety-eight years old and lives in a nursing home in South Dakota. She has grandchildren, great-grandchildren and three great-great-grandsons. When I asked her what she liked to do for her grandchildren, she wrote telling me that she and her husband liked to give money to their grandchildren for college. One time when they were giving out checks, Jim asked her why she gave away all that money. "Because we love you and we want you to remember that," she told him.

When Gladys and Ed moved to town about fifty years ago the previous owners of the house left a shelf full of things. Their children and grandchildren selected what they wanted. Gladys wrote that most of the grandchildren still have the treasures they chose. Gladys wrote, "Some are antiques — but they still like that old stuff — and they always tell people where they came from."

Gladys has always been a magician, making wonders from the ordinary. She calls herself a postage stamp artist. She trims tiny pictures from cancelled postage stamps and creates new miniature collages to decorate notepaper. And still tats — making lengths of lace and lacy ornaments and bookmarks. When she writes to me, this sharp-witted lady cuts out the return address from my previous letter and pastes it on an envelope to me, thus ensuring the accuracy of the address. Last year, when I saw Gladys and I asked her how she was, she bluntly replied, "Well, I ain't getting any younger!" (I think she's getting better.)

Grandmother Sylvia and Grandfather Bill C. have organized their gift giving for their grandchildren. They **give a "rite of passage" gift** for their grandsons when the boys are thirteen years old, a shaving kit filled with toilet articles — shaving cream lotion, aftershave, deodorant, etc. When the girls are twelve years old they have their ears pierced. The girls choose the salon where they will have the piercing done and their new earrings. Grandmother accompanies the girl and her mother.

It began with Judy who wanted her ears pierced but was apprehensive. When the beautician came into the room, Judy started to holler, "I can't see!" Sylvia thought her granddaughter was going to faint so she told her to put her head down and Judy quickly recovered. Grandmother Sylvia is a writer and, true to her bent for writing, she requires each granddaughter to write a story about their ear-piercing experience.

Sylvia says that the sixteenth birthday is the big year. At that time, she gives them each a scrapbook that she has been filling with pictures and memorabilia since they were born. The first page has the child's name, the meaning of the name, the child's birth announcement, baby pictures, the first day of school and on and on. At age 16, Sylvia feels her grandchildren are old enough to save their own mementoes. As the grandchildren grow, they look forward to receiving the gift book of the story of their own life.

Sylvia and Bill have another family tradition for their granddaughters. The girls receive a cedar chest for high school graduation. Someone said, "That is so old-fashioned" and Sylvia's response was "Well, I am an old-fashioned grandmother." In the chest, Sylvia includes a letter "telling them a little about my life, our family traditions and the hope that they will stay close to Our Lord and do the best they can in life. But we will love them regardless of what they accomplish."

Grandfather Bill D. remembers his grandfather promised him a watch for his 21st birthday if he didn't smoke by then. That watch has meant a lot to him over the years. Like other families our family passes down a beautiful pocket watch that belonged to my husband's great-grandfather. My son has it under a glass display dome.

Think of giving a family gift game — I remember sending a wooden game somewhat like foosball. Maybe a carom board will help them recall the memories of your own childhood. Give your child's childhood toys back to your child's child. Cyndi had a Ruthie Revlon doll and with freshened-up clothes the doll became a gift to her daughters. Maybe you're ready to give away your doll dishes or train set or trucks. Or maybe you have a favorite old checkerboard or bag of marbles that would be a remembrance from grandfather.

As your grandchildren get older, **why not give them some of your family treasures?** Think of the cup and saucer sets, the salt and pepper shakers, figurines, old shells and rocks, some of your old jewelry, or grandfather's cuff links. Maybe a grandchild has longingly fingered a paperweight on your desk. Shine it up, find a nice box and include a note telling where and when you got it and how you used it.

Grandparents face other gift-giving challenges with changing times and changing traditions. If you didn't grow up Catholic you often don't know the traditions of First Holy Communion. A Methodist grandmother had a new experience when she was involved with her grandson's bar mitzvah. On the other hand, the religious rituals and gift-giving at a first communion and confirmation, bar and bat mitzvahs may change according to the locale, so grandparents are urged to ask the parents about their expectations.

The Daniel grandchildren receive coin sets as confirmation gifts. These can be for the birth year of the child or maybe for the year of the confirmation. My granddaughters have received special angels as confirmation gifts. It seems harder to find the right gift for boys. A rock found naturally in the shape of a cross became a gift for one grandson.

A Christmas ornament each year for each grandchild is a good idea. When traveling, grandparents can shop for an ornament that is special for the child. A nautical or boat ornament pleases Matthew who has always liked boats. Put the child's name and year on the trinket and when they have homes of their own they will have ornaments with special meanings for their own Christmas trees. Send a tiny decorated Christmas tree to the grandchild in a college dorm or an apartment. Carrie received a little silk Christmas tree from an aunt that was decorated with crisp dollar bills folded into different shapes.

Grandmother Chrys learned a valuable lesson about presents for grandchildren. She told her friends Bill and Betty how much she was looking forward to shopping for her first granddaughter Caitlin — after six grandsons. One Christmas Betty came home with a beautiful dress for their first granddaughter and her husband really called her on the carpet. "Don't you remember how mad you got when my mother bought our little girl a dress for Christmas? You thought my mother thought we couldn't afford to buy our own dresses!"

If you have the resources, you might consider larger gifts, but I recommend that you talk with the parents before you give them. Be sure their parents approve before you give a scholarship to preschool or college, music lessons, art or craft classes or horse riding lessons

When all else fails, give money. Maybe once in awhile you can give money. One year I wrote each grandchild a handwritten letter telling them I wanted their help with my Christmas shopping. I asked each of them to use the cash that I had enclosed, (it's inconvenient for children to cash checks) to buy themselves a gift. They were to wrap it and put it under the tree. I even enclosed a "To _____ from Grandma" gift tag.

I also included a self-addressed stamped envelope with paper that they were to return with their thanks to me, telling what I had given them. This worked pretty well, although one-third did not return the thank you letter and I hardly knew what to do. But later, I told the "non-respondents" I was disappointed that I didn't hear from them. It was really fun to get those letters in January — and February.

Another idea is to give cash and include a certificate of long legalese language of whereases and whereins. Money in their pockets provides great shopping for teenage girls during the after-holiday sales when they can get more for their money. A little pouch of quarters can make magic for children who are going to DisneyWorld or traveling other places. Grandkids in college can always use a roll of quarters for their laundry or vending machines.

I thought I had found the perfect gifts for an eleven-year-old grandson. At the museum I paid a dollar for a geode, a rock which when broken open reveals a crystal cavity never seen by man. And I found a Klutz book showing many different ways to fold a dollar bill. I made a trip to the bank to get eleven one-dollar bills so my grandson would have crisp bills to learn the intricate folds. Imagine my thoughts when I got his thank you note:

Dear Grandma,

Thanks for the spending money. Every Christmas should be this great. Thanks for the geode, too.

> Love,
> Your Grandson

Although I missed the mark that time, books are the best magic-makers of all. Seven-year-old Megan knows that books and grandparents can make a difference. She told her first-grade teacher "My Nana will read anything to me at anytime." Nana Soni says her favorite book is *Poofin*, a Christmas story, and Megan wants to hear it through all seasons.

Reading is the most valuable skill that one can have. In fact, our technology would not exist without the written word. Reading brings mentors, teachers, motivators and amusement makers who have ever written anything directly into our everyday life. Books are dream catchers — they capture and hold the dreams and visions of others so they can be shared and sown like seed to sprout more ideas and dreams for the reader.

One way grandparents or other elders can nurture the love of reading is to introduce the child to the public

library. At our library, anyone of any age may have a library card. The librarian said the only requirement is that the person be present at the library to obtain the card. Even babes in arms can have their own library card in our city.

Charlie Rose of PBS talk show fame related his early experience with the mobile library near his small town of Henderson, North Carolina. "The joy of my life was the coming of the library van...it introduced me to the world, books and learning," he said. Author/historian David McCulloch, who talked with Rose, emphasized that public libraries are the most equalizing influence in our country, providing entrance to a treasury of knowledge in books and frequently now, libraries provide computer accessibility. This information is provided to anyone free of charge. This is real cultural diversity — that current buzzword.

Give the "empty books" to grandchildren suggesting they keep a Lifelong Reading List. Ask the child to record every book and author they read — much as birdwatchers keep Lifelong Bird Lists recording every new bird they see.

In the spirit of Dave Letterman, my grandchildren helped me develop the

Top Eleven Reasons to Give Books for Gifts.

11. Books are cheaper than most toys.
10. Books don't break.
 9. Books don't need batteries.
 8. You don't need a box to wrap it.
 7. It's cheaper to mail a book.
 6. Books are always the right size for the child.
 5. Books can be chosen to fit a child's interests.
 4. Books don't wear out and they are recyclable.
 3. Books build imaginations.

2. Books don't cause tooth decay.

And the number one reason to give books as gifts is:
1. BOOKS ENCOURAGE READING, THE MOST IM-
    PORTANT CONCEPT FOR LIVING.

Whether your grandchildren are affluent or de-prived, as grandparents you can be MAGICIANS and make magic out of the ordinary and "sprinkle stardust in their eyes."

Grandparents Are Cheerleaders

No matter what you do,
your grandmother thinks it's wonderful.
— Judith Levy

eing a CHEERLEADER for our grandchildren is one of the most important tasks for grandparents. Supporting grandchildren in their favorite pursuits, praising them for their individual efforts, cheering them on at their sporting events or quietly standing beside them when things aren't so good — all these ways let grandchildren know that grandparents value and respect them.

Grandparents who affirm and approve of their grandchildren no matter what happens build self-esteem and confidence that will help the child be successful. Spending time doing what the child wants to do builds closeness and trust. Sometimes we do our best, just by being there. A great preacher and inspirational speaker, Dwight Moody, said,

"Lighthouses don't blow horns, they just shine."

Willy's grandparents returned after sabbatical leave for the fall semester at a western university. "What I missed most when you were gone, was having both of you sitting on the sidelines at my soccer game, cheering me on and encouraging me, even when I didn't deserve it," he said. It isn't always easy for twelve-year-old boys to express their appreciation to their grandparents. But when that lack of support and mental conditioning impacts your soccer game a fellah has to admit reality. Willy learned how lucky he is to be growing up in the same city with his grandparents, and a whole bunch of aunts and uncles and cousins who think Willy is great, too.

Soccer, football and basketball aren't the only places for cheerleaders. However, I was shocked to know there are grandparents who show favoritism to children with athletic ability over children with math or computer agility. Grandparents who threaten to stay away from sporting events if kids don't practice and shape up put stress and pressure on the whole family. This is tough on the child's self-esteem as well as on the relationships with the parents. Grandparents are for being cheerleaders not for producing great athletes or for creating computer geniuses.

Another grandma was more encouraging. She said, "We don't go to see Carly win, we go to see her play." Brock Kidd wrote of his grandparents' support in a *Daily Guideposts* meditation. His grandfather promised, "When you play football, I'll be your biggest fan." Kidd was grateful for grandparents "who never give up on us."

Grandparent cheerleaders are watchers, bystanders, spectators, observers, beholders, encouragers and motivators. We begin this role at a very early stage in grandparenting. Some of us are watchers before we are grandparents. We have our eye on things. We watch our daughters and daughters-in-law and sometimes our eagle-eye can spot the glow or the pallor of a new grandchild on the way before the parents can. The role as watchers and observers continues all through a pregnancy and, of course, after delivery.

I'm reminded how much times have changed. My mother's sister and her family moved to Montana in May or June of 1934 shortly after their youngest child was born. But, the story is that my mother didn't tell her sister about her own expected baby and Keith was born on July 3.

If we live near our "infanticipating" children, it is easier to watch and behold this wonderful mystery of human growth. Now our new technology affords long-distance grandparents some of the same awesome feelings. Grandparents display wavy sonograms on their refrigerators. Grandma Dorothy and Grandpa Bud anxiously followed their son and daughter-in-law's pregnancy although they live 300 miles apart. Four months before the birth, Grandma and Grandpa saw (via video on their living room VCR) the steady beating heart of their two-pound grandson in vitro. As he moved around in his warm cocoon, the tiny baby made no attempt to cover his masculinity — a tiny little matchstick confirmed that he would carry on the family name.

It's easy to cheer for a newborn, especially if you are a grandparent who isn't awakened in the night by a colicky cry. As new grandparents we seem to sense the miracle of birth more when it's our own child giving birth than when it happened to us. And we seem to think no one else has experienced the wonder of those precious moments when life begins.

When I picked up the phone and heard the breathless excitement in Idonna's voice, I knew their new grandbaby was here. She continued, "Bob and I were there, in the delivery room this morning, at 3:03 a.m. It was just marvelous. Brenda had an epidural — I couldn't have watched if she'd been in pain. It was so incredible — words just can't express how I felt." She kept on bubbling. "It was a top-of-the-mountain experience and then I heard this beautiful music." I began to wonder a little — music?? "Yes, the beautiful strains of a Brahms lullaby fill the air of the OB ward to welcome each new arrival. This triggered our emotions and our eyes filled with tears. Craig cut the cord and Brenda was so beautiful. She looked directly at the baby and told him, 'You've got two big sisters at home that are gonna love you...and the best daddy...and you're gonna like me, too.'" At that, my friend said she had to make some other calls so she and Bob F. could drive back to Omaha. "That baby needs to see us," she said. "We want him to know we're his grandma and grandpa."

Another grandmother friend also has first hand experiences of the birth of her grandchildren. Grandmother Twila was present in the birthing room when her daughter, who is a surgical nurse in the same hospital, delivered Tessa. Tessa's daddy, not-quite-three-year-old twin brothers Taylor and Tyler and six-year-old Trent were also there. Twila, who is a retired medical technologist, said, "We all know the doctor and when he came in he asked if everyone was there so he could begin. The boys took it in stride. They were climbing up on their mother's bed, anxious to see their new baby sister."

Anymore it seems, if grandparents aren't in the midst of things, they haven't experienced a real grandparent bonding. Grandfather Russ felt ill-equipped for his new role — he thought he needed some sort of training. "I was afraid I'd drop him. He wasn't mine, you know." Later Russ decided it was just like riding a bicycle, "It all came back to me."

I asked a friend what it was like to be a new grandfather. His voice softened and thoughtfully chose his words and said something like, "Holding little Breanna, I could only think of her innocence and the miracle of

how she came to be in my life." Another grandfather
came up and broke the spell, "Your life is never going to
be the same...and your wife is never going to be the
same...and your pocketbook is never going to be your
own again." They both laughed thinking about the dot-
ing grandmothers they are married to.

Respondents to the grandparent survey said they
were thrilled, excited, elated and ecstatic upon becoming
a grandparent. One grandmother said, "I felt as though
a little angel had come into our lives." Another said, "I
had to pinch myself to believe it was true. At once I
became an S.O.G., a Silly Old Grandma." A grandmother said she had attended Lamaze classes with her
daughter since the daddy was in the service overseas.
She said she had mixed emotions since she could only
offer moral support, but "I felt such joy and wonder at
seeing the baby born. I cried and then called and let
everyone know the news." One grandfather said, "I realized how quickly time had passed with our own children." Another grandfather said he was happy and sad;
"happy to have a new little one in the family to watch
grow and develop without the responsibility of raising
him, but I was sad to realize that I was getting old, old
enough to be a grandpa."

Some new grandparents get kind of foxy and frisky.
One said, "I unrolled a roll of shelf paper and wrote 'It's
a Boy' and put it on the fence." A seventy-year-old
grandfather said, "I lost two buttons from my shirt."
Other grandparents put pink or blue balloons on their
mailbox or on the mailbox of the new parents. A grandfather said he went to the school where his wife taught
and while she was outside for recess he wrote the message on the blackboard — "You are a grandmother. By-
ron Jon arrived." One grandmother said, "I was at a
ballgame and I got a little giddy. In fact, I ended up
spraining my ankle." One new grandmother was so ex-

cited about her new grandbaby that, in between phone calls to her friends, she went out into the yard and turned cartwheels. That's what I call being a cheerleader for your grandchild!

Grandparents can make quite a spectacle of themselves cooing and coaxing a grandbaby to smile. But, when we are rewarded with that evanescent grin and intense look directed only at us, a radiance overcomes us and we know that Joy of Grandparenting.

What a joy it is to go to Grandparents' Day at Preschool. Kids put on their best behavior and are eager to share their little life experiences with their significant others. Nothing can compare with their exuberance as you show them by your presence that they are important to you. I remember going to Emilie's Early Childhood Learning Center. I realized that I didn't have to make "cocktail hour small talk" with the other grandparents over our Kool-aid and cookies. My *raison d'etre* was to listen to Emilie's recounting of her achievements and to render appropriate approval and praise. Visiting Claire's preschool, I was the only visitor and received all kinds of extra privileges. Claire was the storyteller for my benefit so I could praise her skills. That's what a grandma is for, to be a cheerleader.

"Watch me," is the watchword of young children. And we grandparents wait patiently for the magnificent feat to be accomplished. I'm told that although Grandfather Don Clifton, CEO of The Gallup Organization, travels extensively he often finds himself playing "watch-me" Nerf basketball with a young grandchild.

Our grandchildren want us to observe and encourage them as they practice their precarious stunts on the monkey bars or swing sets. But, some of the greatest thrills of my grandparenthood have been to participate in their same clever acts. It made Patrick and Claire look even better when I tried to walk with my hands across the parallel bars. However, I had the time of my life remembering my "snow-fun" childhood stuffed into all the warm clothes I could find, as the kids and I went sledding in their backyard. It was another high point in my life as I actually made it to the top of the tree house along with Claire and Patrick.

My friend Chrys wrote that she had spent her winter sitting on a board watching her grandson — in the bleachers at the football games, the basketball games, wrestling matches and track meets. In their South Dakota rural community, there's no question but that board-sitting is the thing for grandparents to do, as long as they are able. The grandchildren know that their grandparents are there rooting for them. The kids do their darndest to make their grandparents proud. They know that their feats will be replayed over and again when the families gather and regroup. The kids also know that their achievements are likely to be retold in the family Christmas letters. That's the job of a grandchild, to make their grandparents proud.

I've learned that grandparents will go to every effort to watch their grandchildren perform. Nana Soni is a cheerleader even though her granddaughters live on the East Coast. She has been known to fly across the country so she can be at Bayleigh's and Megan's dance recital. One proud grandmother planned an extensive 2,000 mile trip by car taking along three other grandmothers to watch Barb's grandson perform as the drum major of his high school.

One fall I was visiting my son and his family and watched Matthew play football. It was worth all the time spent in the freezing rain and wind to see number 76 make some grand plays. I've planned my holiday trips to the West Coast to hear Phillip play in the symphony. It was thrilling, too, to listen in on his rehearsals. While in California, it was also important that I go to Michael's karate class and sit with the fathers, mothers and a couple of grandmothers around the edges. A complete turn-about in mode and mood, I learned that karate, like the symphony, demands discipline and concentration. It's funny how much you learn from your grandchildren.

Patrick, 9, with his first 4-H calf.

I'm lucky to cheerlead for my Nebraska kids frequently. The activities of the Nebraska cousins add a great variety to my life. Carrie's and Emilie's dance recitals in the big theater are major productions, Las Vegas-type shows (after the two- and-three-year-olds in their pink tutus have toddled across the stage and a few of them have tipped over). My granddaughters' piano recitals are held on the university campus where two concert grands face each other on a huge stage.

When I attend piano recitals for Claire, Patrick and Alex I sit on folding chairs in the tiny simple church with a single spinet piano. Their 4-H song and dance performances at the county fairgrounds share space with quilts, pumpkins and squash. My anxiety level rises as I watch the grandkids lead the animals at the beef and swine shows. This year Alex will show a 4-H "bucket calf," an orphan calf that he has fed from a bucket with a big nipple on it. However, it's my grand-parent pleasure to enjoy this medley of performances — football games, the symphony, karate, recitals or county fair. It isn't the location or the price of the costumes that make me feel proud. It's seeing the youngsters doing their best.

And it's my official job to capture those Kodak mo-ments. **Every grandparent should have an easy-to-use camera always loaded and ready.** Double-prints are great souvenirs to share with the grandkids and their parents. You can send the 4X6 prints as postcards.

I recommend an aim-and-shoot 35 mm camera that has an automatic focus and built-in-flash. As you look in the viewfinder, carefully frame the subjects. Look for tree branches, or weird objects in the background that may appear to "grow" out of the subject's head.

Don't be stingy about taking pictures. Professional photographers take several shots anticipating someone will blink their eyes. The cost of a roll of film is a small price for a precious memory. I take a lot of kidding for taking lots of photos. My family complains as the turkey gets cold while I'm taking pictures.

A son-in-law called my attention to a Gary Trudeau "Far Side" cartoon. It pictured a pack of wolves huddled over their prey with a lone wolf nearby with a camera. The caption was something like, "Hey, Gertrude, why do you always have to get that thing out everytime we have a family dinner?"

I have missed some great Kodak moments. It was my job to host the genius of high-speed photography, Dr. Harold Edgerton. "Doc" and his wife Esther re-

I didn't know Alex had a halo until this picture was developed.

turned to their alma mater at the University of Nebraska. As we visited the campus, I carefully framed the old inventor with my camera against the fluffy white clouds, the flowering pink trees and the white cupola of the library. But no one else will ever appreciate that picture, since I forgot to put film in the camera.

Grandparents' gear should also include a video camera and a VCR (videocassette recorder). My neighbor lady phoned one Monday morning to tell me they were home and asked if I wanted to share her "getting-back-to-earth" time by watching the video of her grandson Timmy as Oliver in his fifth grade school production. I hardly know Timmy, but I easily caught her infectious Joy in Grandparenting with her commentary. I agreed wholeheartedly that Timmy is so good looking and he *does* have a beautiful voice.

This grandmother also told me she had found a special gift that was perfect for Timmy's big debut. The "Make-a-Wish" Foundation sold a gold wishing star in a little cloth pouch as a fund-raiser. She told Timmy since he was a (their) star, she wanted him to have it as a remembrance of the occasion. Later, he confided that the star, in the pouch in his pocket, had given him courage on stage when he got nervous. And at the basketball game, he was sure it had helped win the game. At this time, Timmy's grandmother explained that the star was not a magic charm — the star could not make things happen. She reminded him that it was a wishing star and it could simply remind him what his goals were and that his Grandma and Grandpa were always cheering for him.

It was Addie Scheve, Mrs. Nebraska in 1980, who first told me how important it is to have one grandchild at a time. This was the best plan when our three grandsons lived four blocks away while their dad was in Korea. Their mother really needed the relief once in awhile and it was easy for us to have one child at a time. As the boys were older and living in California, it was a good idea that each boy have a special summer after his eleventh birthday with his grandparents. We lived in the city and their other grandparents lived on a Nebraska farm so each boy spent a couple weeks with each pair of grandparents.

John arrived at the airport on a hot summer day after his first plane trip. It was a good grandparent/grandson project to refurbish the Volkswagen we had gotten new the month he was born. We cleaned every square inch of the inside of the "Bug" and spray painted the outside. Mark had his eleventh summer with us, too. He spent time on the farm at his aunt and uncle's. They learned he was better at babysitting than roguing the soy bean field. When Matt arrived for his eleventh summer, I was better organized for his visit. There were swim days with a neighbor boy, household jobs, rockets to build and writing assignments. The few weeks with each grandson proved to be rebonding times and great memories.

A few years later a revised game plan was replayed with two other California grandsons. Eight-year-old Michael and eleven-year-old Phillip came as a pair. We did the tourist bit — going to the top of the Capitol Building and the museums. We discovered the museum preparation rooms and saw rows and rows of dinosaur bones and other fossils. The boys got a taste of Nebraska football when we went to Cornhusker Photo Day. I took their pictures with the big guys and they got autographs. A couple of weeks with grandchildren in your home puts a better perspective on your relationship. After they have gone home with their souvenir photo albums, you realize you really are cheerleaders.

My first grandsons are now young men. Last spring when John and Tanya were married, I felt much like a cheerleader as I joined the line dancers at the reception. But, a prouder performance was dancing with the bridegroom. I also had proud moments visiting Grandson Mark in the U.S. Army on duty at a NATO training base in Europe. Mark had a few days leave and eagerly showed us the travelers' view of his surroundings. I'll never forget the time we spent in Salzburg, the land of *Sound of Music*.

A proud moment dancing with John III at his wedding.

Refrigerator doors in the homes of grandparents become bulletin boards peppered with children's drawings, school papers, newspaper clippings and photographs. Some grandparents have special art creations framed and hung in their living rooms. One grandmother solved her gallery space problem by taping the drawings of the future artist to the walls of her laundry room.

You have seen vehicles with bumper stickers proclaiming "I love my grandchild." My own design-it-yourself sticker, "Ask me about my grandchild(ren)" decorated with hugs ❤s and kisses Xs, has found its way to many cars, pickups, wheel-chairs, refrigerator doors, mailboxes, luggage, retirement home doors and nursing home beds. A young friend suggested the sticker is more than bragging, that it declares a value that increases the grandparents' own sense of well-being.

In *Grandparenting in a Changing World*, Eda LeShan repeats a Puerto Rican saying, "If someone boasts about himself, others say 'I guess he has no grandmother, that's why he has to boast about himself.'"

We are often walking billboards wearing shirts advertising our grandparent status. A friend gave me a red shirt with white letters proudly proclaiming "If I'd known grandchildren were so much fun, I would have had them first."

Gardener Grandma Jackie has a delightful shirt that came from her grandchildren Caitlin and Kendall in Phoenix. Colorful halves of an orange, pear, apple, a pea pod and acorns adorn the insightful message, "Grandchildren are like seeds...in each is a promise of the future. Nurture them with love."

Great things are accomplished when we know someone believes in us. When I am unsure of myself, if someone comes along and encourages me, I can move on and accomplish that endeavor. In the chapter, "Grandparents are Beacons," I tell about a young woman named Dawn. She confided, "If I have a tough week, I just try to hang in there until Friday because that's the day my grandmother prays for me. And then I know everything is going to be all right." Her grandmother provides inspiration for persistence, for hanging in there, a buttress in an unsteady world as well as a legacy of faith. Grandparents, who pray for their grandchildren and tell them, are very much like cheerleaders, except they're less noisy.

"Encourage one another daily," is the exhortation in Hebrews 3:13 (NIV). Fred Bauer wrote of an elderly neighbor who lamented that she couldn't understand "why the Lord is keeping me around." Bauer reminded her that her children and grandchildren still needed her prayers and her support.

There are times when grandparents feel at odds with "the way things are" and don't know how to react or respond. We find ourselves in new situations that conflict with our usual mindset. Eda LeShan tells how her mother resolved the conflict she felt when LeShan's daughter Wendy moved into an apartment with her boyfriend. Despite her Victorian upbringing that disapproved of co-habitation without marriage and a severe heart condition, Wendy's grandmother slowly and deliberately climbed five flights of stairs with gifts of coffeepot, dishes and silverware for a tea party. Why? She said, "It's simple. I love Wendy, she's my grandchild. Nothing must stand in the way of our relationship."

In the midst of our cheerleading exuberance, sometimes we have to practice bending a little in order not to break. We have to stretch our thinking and reach for the highest potential for our dear ones.

Our words of encouragement are meaningful and significant to our grandchildren as they are growing up even though it's not always easy to see grandchildren grow up. Watching a granddaughter blossom into young womanhood or seeing a grandson struggle into manhood can be emotional experiences for grandparents. A good friend said it better, "It's whoops, here they are all grown up." But, seeing the children of my children find their niche in the world with their particular talents makes me happy and proud. This is the real Joy.

Knowing the value of encouragement and motivation for our grandkids, this one task gives purpose to our lives as grandparents. As we grow older, we realize that our grandkids never outgrow their need for a CHEERLEADER and no one can do it better than a loving grandparent.

Grandparents Are Playmates

Grandmothers are just antique little girls.
— an old saying

O f the many hats that grandparents wear, being a PLAYMATE is the favorite. It's really the most fun. Grandchildren often arrive just when we need a break from the serious business of growing older. Then we can pretend that we are young again. We can put on our fishing hats, our baker's hat, our reading spectacles and our dress-up tea party clothes.

In addition to their being our favorite leisure time activity, we learn a lot from playing with our grandkids. We get a glimpse of the world they live in — what they're thinking, what their friends think, what's important to them and what's important to their parents. (They tell us things that are going on their parents would never tell us!)

Grandfathers are noted for wanting to be cronies and pals. Some grandfathers do dangerously defiant things with their grandchildren. In the movie, *Nobody's Fool*, Paul Newman plays a drifter who has been reunited with his small grandson. The first time they are alone together, Newman lets the kid drive his pickup sitting on his lap. Sometimes, in real life it's almost as if grandfathers and grandchildren conspire to outwit the middle generation.

Grandfathers are often the silly ones, too. They tease and say silly things. When Carrie was a toddler, Grandpa sang a little song to her asking over and over, "Whose little girl are you? Whose little girl are you?" And Carrie soon chimed in in perfect rhythm, "Dranpa's!" Until she got a little older and a little wiser and changed her tune and shot back "Dramma's!" Whereupon the whole game changed and grandpa would "catch her" and not let her go until she sang out "Dranpa."

Grandmas often like to play with dolls and give tea parties. Grandma Elizabeth K. plays at pretending and dressing-up and having tea parties when her grand-daughters come to visit. She makes elaborate plans to be the only adult with the children for these little girl games, even encouraging her other daughter to visit at another time. The granddaughters have a new china tea set that is kept at grandmother's house for these special occasions.

My grandkids — including the little boys — loved having tea parties with the tea set Santa Claus brought me long ago. The amber-colored depression-glass dishes came in a box with an 89 cent price tag. I kept them on a kitchen shelf always available when they were little kids. One of my large cream pitchers was the tea pot to heat water in the microwave. Somehow, the kids relished the risk of "hot" tea. By the time the fruit-flavored decaffeinated tea bag had colored the water sufficiently and it was poured into the tiny cups, the tea wasn't really very hot. The girls also delighted in arranging crackers and cheese or slices of orange or apple on the tray of goodies. They usually found some left-over cock-tail napkins to complete the festive occasion. The ritual of the tea party continues even now that the girls are beyond the tea set stage. It's a pleasure to have the girls make tea and serve refreshments for Grandmother.

In *USA Today*, Sandra Simpson LeSourd described an enchanting tea party she and three "inherited" granddaughters planned during a family get-together at Evergreen Farm in Virginia. "On a sunny August afternoon...when the children were restless...I remembered something I always wish I had done for my daughter...a dress-up party with hats and flowers and all the trimmings." LeSourd found fabrics, old jewelry, silk flowers and ribbons to help the girls get "decked out for high tea in the most glamorous outfits we could put together. They all wanted lipstick, blush, mascara and nail polish."

The tea table was set by the front lawn with a long, lacy white cloth and napkins, fresh flowers in a crystal vase. Small demitasse cups marked each place. LeSourd said, "There was something innocent and enchanting and nostalgic about the whole day."

When my children were small, their Aunt Edis invited them to a fancy tea party for our upcoming visit. The anticipation was much of the event, but they still remember the fancy sandwiches, punch and gloves.

I don't know what happened to pig-tailed Janet Sue, my last best doll. My search has become a pilgrimage. (Why is Janet Sue so important to me?) I only know I like my doll collection and have an ongoing doll tea party in a corner of my home. Not too long ago, my daughter gave me Kirstin Larson, a Swedish immigrant doll of the American Doll Collection. The Pleasant Company has other character dolls representing different eras in American life. Kirstin adds to my Swedish traditions as I change her attire for the holidays. It's fun for me to share my dolls with the little tots who come to visit.

Reserve a drawer or shelf at your house for books, games, toys, puzzles and playthings that are age-appropriate for your grandchild. Children love the security of knowing you keep their special playthings for them. They also like to see familiar toys at your house. Watch garage sales for used toys. I found a big bag of wooden alphabet blocks that turned into a real bargain when I realized how costly they are now. Sanitize used toys in the bathtub by adding a little clothes bleach and detergent to the water. A big-wheel is especially intriguing for a preschooler and can be ridden in the basement or back yard. My big kids have fun with the small skateboard that stays in my garage.

A closet full of dress-up clothes in Grandma's spare bedroom can provide the incentive for wonderful theatrical productions, musical revues and circuses. Grandmother Mabel, a favorite long-time teacher, has a tiny stage and curtains in the corner of the basement rec room just for her grandchildren. A selection of hats hangs from a small size hat tree. Hats with plumes and feathers, men's felt hats, straw hats with flowers, farmer's straw hats, beanies, witches' hats and firemen's hats. In a nearby trunk are scarves, skirts, vests, shirts, capes, shawls, neckties, jackets and sweaters. Also at hand are props, everything needed to keep children occupied for hours.

Mabel's method for keeping the kids busy while sparking creativity motivated me to develop a dress-up closet for my grandkids. Every little kid loves to play pretend, but of course, it helped that my oldest granddaughter had a theatrical flair. As a small child, Carrie danced around the house listening to her Robin Hood record with a wreath on her head pretending she was Maid Marion. When she was outside she played with her imaginary playmates, Tommy, Bobby-Doo and Dorothy, who had a red ribbon in her hair. When Carrie was seven and her family moved to another city, she told me Tommy, Bobby-Doo and Dorothy went to California.

Grandparents must realize that imaginary playmates are very real to children. Dr. Violet Kalyan-Massih, professor of child development, says this precious gift of imagination should not be discouraged. When life is so serious with violence at every turn, children need to dream and fantasize and play. In their homes our grandchildren are often over-organized in all the "good" things — sports, music lessons, gymnastics and computers. Grandma and Grandpa's house can be an emotional sanctuary where they are still little kids who like to play.

Since she was the oldest grandchild who frequently came to my house, Carrie kept play alive at our house. One summer Emilie, who likes to write on the computer, wrote a play for the relatives who came for the Carlson Cousins Golf Tournament. The play was "Sleeping Beauty and Snow White Visit the Land of Oz." Obviously, there were two main characters so Emilie and her cousin/best friend Claire could both have starring roles and choose their favorite gowns from the collection of my daughters' old prom dresses. True to the size of the original story character, the Wizard of Oz was little Alex, who wore a magnificent old dance recital costume.

Grandmother Edis and their oldest granddaughter Elizabeth planned a puppet theater via long-distance for a family holiday get-together. Nine-year-old Elizabeth took care of making the puppets and developing the stories while Grandfather Sid made two beautiful puppet theaters to be sure the children had the right equipment. Grandma helped with the curtains that opened and closed with strings. A big job, it was worth it when they saw what a good time their grandchildren had.

Board games, checkers, chess and card games have long been the amusement domain of grandparents and grandchildren. Besides learning strategy and thinking skills of the games and the pleasure, the generations grow in wisdom and relationships just by being together. Mary Costello, a Lincoln, Nebraska, columnist, wrote, "My grandparents taught me to play Crazy Eights...and they explained what caused dew on the grass and fixed me chocolate chip ice cream cones. I felt I was the most important person in the world to them."

Grandmother Christina invented a game, *Poisson*, which is French for fish, to teach French to her granddaughter Catie. She used 3X5 cards to make thirteen sets of four similar objects with French words printed below. For example, she sketched four dolls, four chairs, four apples, four dogs, etc. They played the childhood game of Fish with players asking for a particular set, such as a doll, to complete the asker's "book" of four dolls. Catie not only learned some French vocabulary, she learned about her grandmother's creativity. That her grandmother created the game just for her made Catie realize how much she was loved. And that learning French can be fun.

When his grandchildren came to visit, Pop-Pop Paul was always prepared with simple projects in his woodworking shop. After his death, the grandchildren mentioned their favorite woodworking projects and the lessons they learned from their activities. Kevin, age 13, said, "Philip and I always carved lots of cool animals with Pop-Pop." Eleven-year-old Philip remembered his grandpa's cautious example, "He always used the power tools because we weren't allowed." Monica recalled a "really neat" bird marionette they had made together and added that "he seemed to have more patience with us than a lot of people did."

Pop-Pop Paul shared his woodworking hobbies with other children and youth in his church. Children vied for their turn to work at his woodcraft table at holiday craft sessions and summer vacation Bible Schools. A wooden puzzle manger scene that he designed and manufactured became a fund-raiser for youth groups. At Paul's death, several young mothers expressed their appreciation for the positive influence "The Wood Man" had on their children.

More than fun and silliness, when grandchildren and grandparents play together, there is a sharing of values and qualities of living that last for a lifetime. Grandparents are always demonstrating examples to grow on. It's the little inconsequential things that really matter. **"We're not meant to do great things for God, but small things with great love,"** is the way Mother Teresa put it.

Holidays present opportunities for play activities and passing on family traditions when the generations get together. Grandparents usually have an abundant resource of Christmas cards or greeting cards that they have received. Children can make postcards from the front covers. Or cut the pictures into simple puzzle parts placing each puzzle in its own envelope. Make gift tags for birthday and Christmas presents cut from the greeting cards.

I was apprehensive about suggesting our usual dyeing of Easter eggs to Patrick and Alex since they were such big guys of nine and eleven. But they got into it with the mixing of colors as they dipped the eggs in one shade after another. They were intrigued watching the hues deepen with the length of time the eggs were left in the dye.

My own creativity surprised me. I put a white paper towel in the egg carton to absorb the extra dye. When I took the towel out, I discovered a whimsical watercolor painting that appeared to be two rows of pastel-colored bunny rabbits! The dye on the paper towel nestled in the bottom of each egg cup formed the bunny body and the ears came from the color caught on the sides of the egg section. I was so proud of my masterpiece I put it on the refrigerator door!

Halloween is a fun time for kids and grandparents. If they live in the same area, kids know that they can get special treatment when they go trick or treating at grandma and grandpa's house. Carrie was at our house one day the fall she was five. She said, "Grandma, if you bend down, I'll whisper in your ear what I'm going to be for Halloween if you promise not to tell a single soul, not even your mom and dad." Of course, I promised secrecy and Carrie confided she was going to be a fairy princess. Remembering her cute costume from last year, I said, "Oh, you were such a good witch last year, and your costume probably still fits you, why not be a witch again?" With a knowing look, Carrie flatly denouced the idea, "Oh, Grandma, you'd recognize me!"

Delightful encounters with these dear, naive children brighten and lighten our days. From experience, we know how important it is to be prepared for their visits. And when we are in their homes, we need to provide opportunities for a close relationship to grow. A young grandson made that point clear when he talked to his Grandpa Gene on the phone about his upcoming visit. He said, "I want some good one-on-one time with you, Grandpa."

Cody knows the importance of grand-togetherness, too. In late summer, he keeps watch on the plum thicket on their farm. When the plums are ripe he calls Grandma Chrys to tramp with him through the woody areas to gather the wild fruit. Cody helps Chrys prepare and cook the fruit to make jelly. He brings the jelly glasses up from the basement and works right along with her. The jars of ruby-red jelly become special gifts for Cody's favorite teachers and to satisfy the sweet-tooths of his great-grandmothers.

Small children love to play with dough. Do you remember having a handful of bread dough to play with when you were little? A bag of frozen bread dough, thawed, can keep toddlers happy for a long time. School-age children can become experts in rolling or patting out the dough, dabbing on some butter or margarine, sprinkling sugar and cinnamon and making and baking real cinnamon rolls. What a treat to share and what pride the kids develop with their own accomplishments!

You may not always want to "bake." But a little preparation with a simple play dough recipe can provide many hours of kneading, rolling and shaping of all sorts of "stuff."

♥x♥x♥x♥x♥x♥x♥x♥x♥

Play Dough

1 1/2 cups of salt
3 cups of flour
3 cups of water (add a few drops of food coloring)
6 teaspoons cream of tartar
    (this keeps it from getting sour)
3 tablespoons cooking oil

Mix all the ingredients together in a large skillet. Cook over low heat, stirring constantly until mixture comes together into a ball and cleans the pan — like when mixing pie dough. Cool and knead until it is pliable. Store in a plastic container in the refrigerator. This will keep 2 to 3 months. Let it warm to room temperature before using. Since these are all food ingredients, a taste of the play dough will not hurt a child, however, it should not be considered food. Large quantities would be harmful.

To make ornaments, eliminate the oil in the play dough recipe. Push an ornament hanger or yarn into the top before it dries. After the ornament dries, you can paint it with poster paints.

If your toddlers cannot resist putting things in their mouths, you might try Peanut Butter Play Dough. Just be sure they wash their hands before you start.

♥x♥x♥x♥x♥x♥x♥x♥x♥

Peanut Butter Play Dough

1/2 cup peanut butter
1/2 cup nonfat dry milk
1 tablespoon of honey

Knead the ingredients until pliable and workable. This will stay fresh if you store it covered in the refrigerator. Kids can model figures or use cookie cutters to make their favorite shapes.

Have you ever tried fingerpainting with shaving cream? If you don't mind the messies, spurt shaving cream on a counter top or a large piece of slick paper. Go to it — talk about the difference in textures. A few drops of food coloring can make it more interesting.

When the children come to your house, you may find you need extra glasses for milk, juice and soft drinks. Keep disposable plastic glasses or foam cups on hand. Write the name of each child on the cup with a crayon or grease pencil. The short fatter cocktail glasses are less likely to tip over. **When the children are very small, outlaw red, purple and orange drinks in your household.** This eliminates stains on table cloths, carpets, or Formica. Lemonade, apple and white grape juice are good, but it's wise to wipe up the spills to eliminate the stickies. Sugar spills on tablecloths or carpet will turn brown with age.

Be sure to keep lots of bandage materials (there are some charming "kid-designer" strips) and antiseptic cream on hand for the inevitable scratches and bumps. A red washcloth can save a lot of tears. Washing off a cut finger with a red washcloth is almost fun and the child is not frightened at the sight of the blood on the washcloth. Of course kisses always make it better and a little extra pampering from a grandparent is a sure cure.

Some grandchildren suffer from migraine headaches — a frequent problem in our hurried, hectic, high-achieving culture. One little girl's parents left specific instructions for medication and couch-rest when she went to spend the evening with grandma. Grandma didn't listen too well but went ahead with her plans including the little girl in their familiar games and activities. All evening the granddaughter was bright and perky — her usual self. When the parents arrived to pick their daughter up, the little girl immediately reverted back to her sick-child syndrome seeking her parents' sympathy. Grandmother reviewed the evening, telling about the good times they had together and the child couldn't keep quiet chattering on about the fun she had had. The father put his arm around his daughter and summed up his thoughts, "I think Grandma was good medicine."

Modern technology isn't always the solution. Sometimes the old ways are better by their simplicity. Although children have access to computers in their homes and schools, an old typewriter can be a fascinating toy for a child. It isn't mysterious or magical. When a child touches a typewriter key, he can actually see the letter being imprinted on the paper. The child knows that he or she made it happen. Old typewriters show up at garage sales for little or nothing.

Children love to have their very own flashlight. Let your overnight grandchildren have a flashlight to read their books after you've kissed them goodnight. They feel in control and less fearful of being in a strange bed and hearing strange noises. Nightlights or dimmed lights help, too. The batteries in the flashlight may wear out very quickly, but that is a small price to pay for your grandchild's feelings of security.

A piece of cellophane tape on the fingers of a small child can keep him or her occupied for quite a while. You might try it for the toddler in a high chair at a restaurant. This is also a good diversion during a photo session. Grandma Edis recommends tape, stickers, little notebooks and crayons for "survival" packets for little ones at special dinner parties to keep them busy while the adults linger a little longer to visit.

Diversions such as day trips to museums, zoos and parks rate high with both grandparents and grandchildren. Many towns and cities have delightful museums and zoos that incorporate hands-on-activities allowing the kids to explore and learn while they are entertained. In our city the old zoo has been renovated to be an indoor children's play area. Grandparents need to remember good walking shoes and to plan rest times with light snacks. You can make your grandchild proud if you let him or her have the camera and take pictures of you with the monkeys or on the fire engine.

It's a good idea to use the buddy system if you have more than three or four grandchildren. And when it's time to go home, be sure to count noses. Grandmother Mabel had led many tours for schoolkids to the museum and she thought it would be a snap to take her ten grandchildren. After the family got back home, the telephone rang. It was the museum. It seems one grandchild was forgotten.

Exploring the wonders of nature has always been a great way for generations to develop close ties and a love of the great outdoors. Grandpa Gordon has relished thirty-two summers with his family vacationing in Colorado. About a dozen years ago, it dawned on him that he could help nourish and cultivate this love of the natural world for his grandchildren. Since then, he has presented his grandchildren backpacks for their third birthdays. When summers come around in Colorado, all these young hikers now tug at his pants to "get on the trail."

Grandpa Gordon told Kerri and Rob, when they were but three and four, about his morning vacation ritual. "I always feel so good when I'm in Colorado that each day I go out on the deck or find the largest boulder I can find, get up on it and sing as loud as I can, 'Oh, what a beautiful morning.'" Since then, Gordon says, all "the kids seldom let a morning pass that they don't greet the day in a like fashion. And on the trail, there's seldom a large boulder that they don't climb upon and sing, 'Oh, what a beautiful morning.'"

Grandpa Culver's kids Colorado experiences are not limited to hiking. They fish for trout, hunt for edible mushrooms; learn about wildlife, wild flowers, hummingbirds and the quiet of the forest. They go tubing, play horseshoes and enjoy meals around a campfire. They have adopted a unique pine tree on one of their favorite trails and in between their visits, they inquire about the welfare of their "picnic tree." Grandpa Gordon is proud to have planted the seeds for this regard and respect for the environment. And it didn't take a lot of persuading to convince Sid, Gordon's new wife, to join the Culver Colorado Crew.

Grandparent/grandchild camps are a unique addition to the grandparent arena. Connie Chung on "CBS Nightly News" talked about "Vacations that skip a generation." Under the guidance of the Foundation for Grandparenting, for more than ten years Dr. Arthur Kornhaber has directed camps exclusively for grandpar-

ents and grandchildren from five to eighty-five at Sa-
gamore Lodge in the Adirondacks. Kornhaber developed the camp idea for long-distance grandparents or
for those who seldom see their grandchildren. The camp
format is low-key, encouraging interaction between the
generations. Group activities include swimming, boat-
ing, sports, crafts, singing and square dancing. Afternoons grandparents have quiet talk about their grandkids while the children have other directed activities.
This is a place where special memories keep coming.

Our church has held grandparent/grandchild day-
camps for the past several years. We play paper and
pencil games and sing on the bus. When we went to a
county historical museum, Brittany saw a photo of her
grandmother as a little girl standing with her chums in
front of their rural school. Ruby B.'s granddaughter
spotted the name of an ancestor on an autograph quilt.

Other times grandparents and grandchildren made
family flags, had parades and created crafts together.
Last year each grandparent/grandchild pair or group
had Polaroid photos taken. Then we made frames from
popsicle sticks and decorated them for the photos. Our
group has gone to state parks, local parks, historical
parks and museums. We have roasted hot dogs, ordered
pizza and eaten at the camp mess hall. Grandparents
appreciate a time that is planned for them to be with
their grandchildren without worries of driving and the
security of having other adults around. Grandchildren
look forward to different activities that are planned just
for them and their grandparents.

**Traveling with grandchildren is the ultimate play
time.** Disneyland, DisneyWorld and all the theme parks
provide a perfect playground for affluent grandparents.
Disney sponsors The Big Red Boat, a cruise for grandparents and grandchildren in connection with a trip to
DisneyWorld. Travel agencies are catching on and de-

veloping tours for grandparents and grandchildren. GRANDTRAVEL, a division of The Ticket Counter in Chevy Chase, Maryland has offered domestic and international tours since 1982. Providing tour guides and teacher-trained escorts, GRANDTRAVEL helps grandchildren understand the sites and attractions and assists grandparents with supervising the children. The escorts are on hand to find a dentist for a loose orthodontic wire or to fill a prescription or offer suggestions for homesickness.

Regional travel agencies as well as bank and hospital travel groups for seniors also plan special trips for grandparents and grandchildren. In the Midwest, trips to Binney-Smith's Crayola Factory and Hallmark Cards in Kansas are popular destinations. Goodlife Tours sponsors a bus tour for grandparents and grandchildren. The travelers have videos and games on board and the tour culminates with a covered wagon ride and chuck wagon dinner reminiscent of the prairie pioneers. FUN TOURS specializes in tours to Branson and have a trip organized to please both grandparents and grandkids.

Dude ranches and river float trips appeal to active grandparents. The National Wildlife Federation Conservation Summits (800-245-5484) are weeklong programs led by naturalists with seminars, field trips, square dances, singalongs and recreation of all sorts. Elderhostel, which provides year-round life-long learning (usually on college campuses), has summer and winter programs for grandparents and their grandchildren. Elderhostel provides a neutral zone for the generations to share, experience and have fun without other pressures. If you're not on the mailing list for Elderhostel, call (617) 426-7788 (not toll-free) to obtain a catalog of their many listings.

Plan your trip with your grandchildren before you leave home. The 500-mile drive to the Grandparent/Grandchild Camp in Oklahoma, with my three granddaughters who were eleven, twelve and fifteen was making me a little nervous. I asked advice from all my friends as to their suggestions for the rules of the road. The girls, their parents and I talked about some of the problems we might encounter. Could we agree on the radio stations to listen to? (They each decided to take their own radio.) How would we decide where to eat? How much should the girls spend on snacks and souvenirs? Since there were four of us, who would be stuck sleeping with grandma? Sharon, a school counselor and grandmother, suggested that I let the kids make up the rules for the road.

With much trepidation, I let them. "The Oklahoma Compromise" worked great! The girls seemed to love the challenge. I think they liked being respected enough to make their own rules. There was a copy for each of us and we signed each other's copies before we left home.

The Compromise covered almost everything and some I hadn't thought of.

Finding the Joy of Grandparenting is a little like pursuing the butterfly of happiness — the more you chase it, the more it eludes you. But if you savor the innocence and nostalgia of being a PLAYMATE with your grandchildren, that Joy will find you and settle in your heart.

OKLAHOMA COMPROMISE

1) Anyone wishing to use another person's property must ask before using it.

2) No whining, crying, screaming, hitting, slapping, biting, pinching, kicking, or any other kind of violence will be allowed.

3) No snottiness, sassiness, or sarcasm toward Grandma will be allowed.

4) The person in the passenger's seat controls the radio.

5) Room rotations will be made every night. Everyone will room with everyone else at some time.

6) Car seat rotations will be made every stop.

7) All rotations will be made in this order: Carrie, Emilie, Claire.

8) No messy foods will be allowed in the car. Non-messy food will be allowed.

9) Everyone is allowed to have a carry-on bag. If it doesn't fit in the bag, it doesn't go.

10) Each person has a right not to give out their own food and personal items.

Grandparents Are Kinkeepers

Not to know what has been transacted
in former times is to be always a child.
— Cicero

One of the most meaningful roles for grandparents is that of being a family historian or KINKEEPER, as I prefer to call it. Grandparents are living history and may be the only book grandchildren read that provides a sense of family continuity. Whenever an elderly person dies, it's as though a library burns down and the grandchildren lose that connection with the past.

Family psychiatrist Arthur Kornhaber describes the grandparents' role of historian as living ancestor, family archivist, a link to the past and a time machine. He cites Dr. David Gutmann's depiction of grandparents as "the wardens of culture." In *A Book for Grandmothers*, Ruth Goode writes "They (grandchildren) give us continuity...they link us to the future."

We all need the security of roots. Kate Greer, editor of *New Choices for Retirement Living*, writes, "I like having a history. It's the wonderment of having lived long enough to be able to savor relationships, perceive patterns and see some effect of one's exisitence...Looking back, to my way of thinking, is half of how you figure out how to go forward." Friend Chrys says, "It's like using a rear-view mirror when you are driving."

To know who you are is to know where you came from — who your family is and what your family is about. According to the late psychologist Erik Erikson, the task of identity formation must be accomplished by an individual before one can have healthy close relationships. Youth and family ministers Jerry and Jack Schreur say "Teenagers struggle to build a sense of identity. Unless they understand where they came from and how they fit in, they will have difficulty deciding where to go."

This chapter is about the who, what and how of kinkeeping — of passing on the culture of the family. Some say **who** the family is — or the definition of family — has changed. The legacy that our grandparents give us is the **what** and the means that we transmit our family culture to our grandchildren and their descendants is the **how**.

The bonds between generations can be found even when there are missing links. My professor and friend Ruby G. and her husband have an adopted grandson of Korean parentage. Because Ruby and Glen realized the importance for Patrick to know about his own culture, they traveled to Korea with Friendship Force, an international exchange group. Ruby and Glen absorbed Korean culture while living with a family for a few weeks. After returning home, Ruby tutored a young Korean woman and became friends with the family. Patrick has learned to appreciate his heritage through his adoptive grandparents.

Yes, family circles have changed. Now, the definition of family isn't restricted to biological kin or legal relatives. A survey by sociologists Andrew Cherlin and

Frank Furstenberg, Jr., reveals that one-third of the grandparents have at least one stepchild in the family. Grandparents now have extended families that include half-siblings, significant others, girl friends and boy friends who are the biological parents of their grandchildren and children of the girl friends and boy friends who are not genetically related.

Other families get more complicated. Recently my cousin wrote "Guess I'm still going to be grandmother to Brent's stepchildren despite the divorce...I hear from them oftener than I do from him, so guess I'm the 'good' that was in the family." Chatting with a friend one day she told me of her son's divorce. The ex-daughter-in-law's child (her son is his stepfather) very much wants to continue to be their grandchild. My friend said she is not anxious to stay in touch with the ex-daughter-in-law, but she truly cares for the young boy.

The advice that Ann Landers gave years ago is still appropriate. She said children in stepfamilies are fortunate if they have more than their share of grandparents. Children of divorce have so much pain and stress in their lives that they need all the grandparenting given to them. The investment of any elders' love for a child brings greater rewards than the original cost.

What do grandchildren gain from a grandparent relationship? In the research survey for my master's degree, I asked grandparents what they remember about their own grandparents. Several grew up with a grandparent in the home or lived in the grandparents' home following the death of their mother. They told of the caring and unconditional love they received; only three or four mentioned not liking their grandparents. Several spoke of the quilts and handwork their grandmothers created. Most have fond memories of the food they enjoyed at grandmas' houses. Sugar cookies, cinnamon rolls, German kolaches, Scandinavian kringler, lemon pies, angel food cake and Jello were frequent responses. Grandfathers sometimes cooked, too, but more frequently they handed out candy treats. One man who was a sickly child said his grandfather read to him and "Then as I got older, I would get library books for him."

Recently, Karla, a young mother with a serious chronic illness told her grandmother's story of coming to America at age five with her parents after the Bolshevik Revolution. Drinking poisoned water in Russia caused the death of her grandmother's grandparents. Karla said she gains strength and faith as she recalls the hardships her grandmother endured. She appreciates her own warm bathroom as she remembers her grandmother's tales of cold, outdoor toilets.

Traditional foods and the rituals and customs of mealtimes bind us together as families. Dr. Paul Meier and Paul Thigpen wrote, "Just as each thread delicately woven into a magnificent tapestry adds color and texture, customs celebrating shared experiences also add color to a family's life. Traditions enrich and strengthen families by giving comfort and security to those who carry on the rites."

The good thing is that each family group doesn't have to do everything exactly as their family of origin. As each clan develops their own variation of customs, the group is strengthened.

Although I didn't consider our neighbors' custom of doughnuts for Sunday night supper as nutritionally sound, I'm sure those four grown-up girls have fond memories of their aunts and uncles dropping by each week.

It is important for grandparents to be there in the beginning of the new families, for weddings, of course, and for births, another powerful, sacred moment. Grandparents try to be at the hospital when the birth of a grandchild is imminent. Grandmothers carry cellular phones during their workday when they're expecting grandbabies.

Grandmothers and grandfathers who are Lamaze coaches experience a bonding that occurs among the three generations in those first hours of life. One young grandmother told of delivering her own granddaughter in the bathroom while her thirteen-year-old son called 911. This grandmother maintains a special bond with the now-six-year-old although her ex-son-in-law has custody of the child in another city.

Most grandparents are there for events like baptisms and christenings to celebrate with the whole family. Grandparents often take responsiblity for the apparel worn by the special child. A friend said she purchased the baptismal clothing for each of her grandchildren. Some take great pride in providing heirloom clothing whether it is fragile, antique lace; filmy, frothy nylon of the '50s; or a sensible cotton knit of the '90s. Pieces of an ancestor's christening dress may be laid on the babe's chest for the significant moment only.

It was a lovely experience to create a christening dress for my first granddaughter. Since then other grandbabies have worn it and I'm pleased that Grandma Joyce, from another branch of the family, asked to borrow it for their Rebecca. I hope the names and dates of all the babies who have worn the dress are noted, or perhaps embroidered on the hem making it an authentic family heirloom.

Many grandmothers have established traditional "welcome baby" gifts for each grandchild. Luella made an embroidered prayer sampler, an apple crib quilt and a large stuffed bear for each of her six grandchildren.

Birthdays also top the list for family celebrations — especially for the very young and the very old. The thrill of finding that special present for a little one is one of the Joys of Grandparenting. In the chapter, "Grandparents

Are Magicians" I suggested some unique gifts, not the latest toys advertised on Saturday morning cartoons or found at the discount stores.

Grandparents who live near their grandchildren are lucky if they can party together. Some grandparents make a special birthday date with the birthday child. You can also send a birthday party in a box — tiny favors, treats, several small gifts, napkins, plates, banners and hats. One grandmother had a birthday party for her long-distance grandchild. She videotaped herself singing "Happy Birthday" and playing silly games and chatting with her grandchild.

One of my favorite family celebrations was to attend my grandson's wedding. What a joy it was for six grandparents to be included in that wonderful, traditional occasion! In fact, we elders almost stole the show.

Old family rituals and tradition come out in full force at Christmas and holiday times. Feelings rise to the surface when a new family is born. It's hard to decide where to go and what the holiday foods will be. "What do you mean you have chili for Christmas Eve? Everybody has their big turkey dinner then." "Why on earth do you want to wait to open presents on Christmas morning?" "Whoever heard of having oyster stew for New Year's?"

When families are young, it's easier to be alone in your home to establish your own holiday rituals. After eight years of marriage, we moved to Nebraska and by virtue of necessity, had our first Christmas alone. Our little kids were excited about staying up late and going to church at eleven o'clock. Since my husband and I wanted to sleep in on Christmas morning, we established the tradition of having Santa Claus arrive while we were at church. (That required some creativity.) In later years, a movie in the afternoon of Christmas Eve "took up time" and diffused the agony of waiting for the glorious evening. Now, my son's family carries on the Christmas movie tradition.

Grandparents have to be sensitive to the struggle young parents have in finding their own traditions. Meier and Thigpen remind us that "Christmas is about relationships which means compromise...give-and-take." We don't always have to have our family together on the day, or at the same place. Daughters-in-law bitterly complain about always having to go to his relatives because "We can't disappoint Mother." The mother and mother-in-law relationship can be greatly enhanced if grandmothers will yield to new options. New family traditions can open new doors to understanding.

Grandparents are living ancestors and time machines. Those homespun yarns and tales of yore, whether they are fact or fiction, myth or legend, must be retold so that our grandchildren will know that precious sense of belonging to a group, a clan, a tribe. In the oral tradition of the preliterate culture of hunters and gatherers, tribal elders were valued for their widom. For example, the elders knew how to choose wood for cooking fires or for sustaining the fire for long periods. Some say we are again hunters and gatherers as men and women go out from their dwelling places each day to keep their homes safe and gather sustenance.

According to Dr. Arthur Kornhaber when you pass on family ways, rites and rituals, you teach your grandchildren to think in terms of "we" as well as "I." A child who thinks in terms of "we" feels part of the historical continuum and feels secure and rooted to the past and also part of the present and future. We need this collection of lessons learned through the generations and stories of familial pride. Tales of our ancestors tell about feats of strength, faith, courage, persistence and intuition to continue family virtues. Grandparent yarns tie us together as a family.

I remember writing about Grandpa Rosenquist's faith for a freshman college composition class. The moral of the story as I remember hearing it was that Grandpa never worked on Sunday. No matter what the weather or season, he always hitched up his team and took his family to the little white church on the hill about three miles north of the farm. One hot, summer Sunday morning, they drove past their golden field of wheat that was ripe for the harvest. His neighbor, getting his McCormick Deering reaper ready in the field across the road called out to him, chiding him for not taking advantage of the sunny, dry weather to cut the grain.

Nils kept on driving to Sunday services. That night, a terrible wind and rain storm raged through the prairie and the beautiful grain crop was destroyed. However, the story goes on that the very next year, when a bad hailstorm came through the area, the line of destruction stopped in the middle of the road, leaving Grandpa Rosenquist's fields untouched by the pelting drops of ice.

I can't remember when I first heard the story or who told me. But, Grandpa's strong belief in a loving, just God has always stayed with me and it is reinforced each time I go back to the New Home Lutheran Church Cemetery and see the plaque that commemorates all of my grandparents as founders of that little white church. The building is no longer there. The congregation built a new structure in town. That hilltop cemetery where five generations of my family are buried gives me a great sense of faith, comfort and peace. I have told my children of my plans to use the one space left in the family plot for my burial. I don't consider this morbid or gloomy. Last summer my daughter and grandkids, my niece and her kids giggled while having my picture taken on top of my grave site.

Family rituals, stories and coined phrases that become a part of each household portray our unique values and remind us that we are family. Little kids love routines and games played over and over. Children seldom forget their first table prayer or their bedtime prayer. Grandmas like Waunda encourage their great-grandchildren to learn table prayers and Luke and Jesse proudly respond. Unknowingly, the little boys are showing respect and honor to one of their favorite people.

Lullabies and grandmother songs linger in memories forever. Neighbor Jackie makes up her own words to the tune of "Bell Bottom Trousers." Her grandmother's song goes something like, "Grandma loves Elizabeth/ Grandpa loves her too/ Mommy loves Elizabeth/ Daddy loves her too// Now it's time to close your eyes/ Close your eyes of blue/ Tomorrow we'll go sledding/ Toodle-Oodle-Ooo//" Jackie says the kids keep asking for their own song even when they've grown too big for laps.

A small newborn was fighting for his life in an isolette. The new mother was nervous and scared. Grandmother Joyce arrived and they went to the preemie nursery together, both anxious and worried. The little momma needing comfort asked her own momma to sing the songs she used to sing. So they stood holding each other. The new gramma sang all the old lullabies to her tiny grandson and his mother there in the neonatal unit. It must have worked — grandmother still sings to the sturdy young boy.

Each family wants to know that their family is smarter, stronger, more clever, more talented, better-looking and tougher than any others. Then, we know we can make it through the tough times. In *Black Sheep and Kissing Cousins*, Elizabeth Stone writes,

> Like all cultures, one of the family's first jobs is to persuade its members they're special, more

wonderful than the neighboring barbari-
ans...Attention to the stories' actual truth is
never the family's most compelling consideration. Encouraging belief is. The family's survival depends on the shared sensibility of its
members.

Family stories told over and over reinforce family
values. Grandfather Gordon is a retired professor of
education and his retelling of this family story to his
grandchildren illustrates the family's strong sense of the
significance of education. While Gordon was working
toward his doctorate and teaching at the university,
Stephen, about five, was at home with his mother, playing. The sirens of firetrucks prompted Stephen's question, "Mama, do firemen go to school?" His mother said
yes, firemen go to school. Next, Stephen asked, "Mama,
do policemen go to school?" And his mother said yes,
policemen go to school. Then, the little boy asked,
"Mama, do garbagemen go to school?" With finality in
her voice, his mother said, "Stephen, you're going to
find that anyone who wants to be somebody has to attend school." The little boy had the last word, "Mama,
isn't it most about time Daddy was somebody?"

**How do we pass on traditions, rituals, customs
and culture to the next generation?** Families find ways
that have particular meaning for themselves. Grandparents have many choices as they convey that sense of
family. They may compile genealogy records, write family history, cultivate ethnic heritage, develop family
cookbooks, tour birthplaces, visit parishes and cemeter-
ies of ancestors, read historical novels in the era of forefathers, identify old photographs, document current
family events via videotapes, record stories of elders on
cassette tapes and/or videotapes and organize family
reunions.

Genealogies and family histories take many forms according to the likes and wants of the families. Genealogy is the accurate record of the births, deaths and marriages, where they took place and the names of the family members. My cousin Evelyn and her son Kenn created a marvelous genealogy for the Carlsons. They researched the family records and wrote to relatives for updated information on new babies, marriages and divorces. Computer software helped them keep the records. Kenn developed a form for each family unit. Evelyn and Kenn's materials were melded with photos and stories in time for the Carlson Reunion which marked the 100th anniversary of our grandparents' marriage.

Kenn also put this genealogical information into the form of a Carlson Calendar. The daily calendar gives the name and year of birth for all the known ancestors, siblings, descendants and their spouses who were born on that day. My grandparents, August and Ida Carlson, have more than 200 direct descendants at this writing.

The Church of Jesus Christ of Latter-Day Saints, also called the Mormon Church, holds extensive genealogy records in the center of their organizaiton at Salt Lake City, Utah. Mormon Family History Centers in cities around the country have extensive data banks making their records available using Personal Ancestral File software. The Church of Latter Day Saints provides forms and methods of research at nominal fees to those who request it. Look in your local telephone directory for more information. At the end of this chapter you will find additional information to help you get started on family genealogy.

Family histories take many shapes. Some people want formal, organized materials dotting every "I" and crossing every "T." Other folks are happy with more casual stories, loosely connected that give the "flavor" and feelings of the family. A friend said the old tales are the meat on the bones of genealogy. Family histories can be bound inexpensively at copy centers. If you want several copies printed, inquire at your local print shop.

My part in the Carlson Family History Book was to collect stories and pictures of the families of the seven children of August and Ida. I gathered memories and biographical information from my cousins about their parents. Their stories revealed the hard tales of survival as well as endearing accounts.

Cousin Irene, the oldest grandchild, wrote about her mother, Hilda. "She loved raising poultry of all kinds. In the fall when the turkeys, ducks and chickens were marketed, that money bought our winter clothing — long underwear for everybody, sweaters, overshoes and blankets. Life was uneventful, times were hard and no luxuries as we couldn't afford them, but we were rich that we had each other and were blessed with good health, no operations, no broken bones, no glasses, just childhood diseases that generally hit you in March."

One of the younger cousins, Ida Louise, wrote about her mother Elna. "I know a very central core of me as a person was molded by my mother and her family. Love of family, loyalty, high moral standards and faith in God all were ideals Mother lived by and gave to us. We had her for a few short years as she died young, but her courage in facing death is very real to me still." Sadly, Louise also died when she was still young.

Norman wrote about his dad, Oscar, who was an avid baseball fan. One day Uncle Oscar and Aunt Ruth were sitting in church while the World Series was on radio. Aunt Ruth leaned over and whispered, "I bet I know what you are thinking about." Oscar whispered back, "Shucks, I don't even care who wins."

It was years after my mother's death that I found a collection of short descriptions of my mother's ancestors. Apparently, Aunt Hilda and Uncle Carl wrote down some of the stories and genealogical information as my grandmother and grandfather told them. As far as I know, this is the only written record of these ancestors. Interestingly, the date of this early family history was the year I was born.

My grandmother's great-grandmother was Karin who was born in the late 1700s. One of her stories took place when Sweden was at war with Denmark. Some Danish soldiers entered the room and took her daughter Ingrid out of the cradle and threatened to throw the baby into the fire. Karin told the soldiers to "mind their own consciences." They returned the baby to her safely.

Included in this Rosenquist treasury is a report of the "Feudal System in Skane, Sweden" as described by Grandfather Nils. He said the life of the tenant farmer was hard. If the overlord called the tenants to work they dropped their spoons if they were at meals and hurried to the estate, since the latecomers had the hardest work to do. In my great-grandfather's time, he loaded hay with his hands — wooden hayforks were a later invention.

This record of family names, dates and stories proved invaluable when some of us toured Sweden. I felt transported to the past as we found some of the actual houses where my grandparents had lived. It was thrilling to see the ancient fonts where my forebears were baptized and walk among their burial places.

Old black and white pictures photocopy very well and are more economical than having them reproduced. In fact, it is a good idea to have photocopies made of color photographs — especially wedding photos and family photographs. Color photos of the '60s and '70s often fade. Photos kept under plastic may deteriorate. Having good photocopies made will preserve your family photo history. A friend said copies made of some of her family documents were better than the originals.

Photograph albums are family histories, too. Keep some of the outtakes. Years later it's fun to review the "bad" pictures. Remember the press photograph of First Lady Barbara Bush who was photographed with her granddaughter. Mrs. Bush was smiling graciously for the journalists — completely unaware that her granddaughter was sticking out her tongue and making a horrible face. There have been times when our children have been paging through the family albums and they

THE FAMILY CIRCUS®   **By Bil Keane**

5-31

Copyright 1988
Cowles Syndicate. Inc

"Gee, Grandma, you sure look a
lot different when you wear a
wedding gown!"

REPRINTED WITH PERMISSION OF
BIL KEANE, GRANDFATHER OF 8.

have more fun seeing the not-so-perfect photos. They laugh at the growing stages when they were "fat and ugly."

While developing my husband's family history, I wrote to his aunt by marriage and inquired about family stories. Since Uncle Vernon was deceased and they had no children, she sent a wonderful photograph of a family reunion taken in the 1890s and a typed listing that identified each person. That photo was copied and included in the family history. We also received a copy of Grandmother Agnes's handwritten life story.

As she was nearing her 90th birthday, Grandmother Agnes wrote her story in a little black book. My daughters tell me this story reads like *Little House on the Prairie* books. I have learned that Grandmother Agnes actually lived in the town of Burr Oak, Iowa, at the same time Laura Ingalls Wilder did. Agnes was seventeen and lived on a farm while Laura was ten and lived with Ma and Pa Ingalls in a hotel that Pa managed for a time.

This precious chronicle details how Agnes decided to live with the Davises after her mother died. "I was about seven years old when one bright spring day I was called from play to meet a young man and his wife who lived at Burr Oak. They had a good home and no children. They had heard of me, a child in need of a home. They told me about their house, school, playmates and a mother cat and two kittens. And that I could be their girl and call them Pa and Ma."

Her birth father remarried a couple of years later and asked her to leave her adoptive parents and go with them to Nebraska. "My father was a kind man and loved his family and he did not want to leave me." Agnes wrote, "Again I was asked to make my own decision. I was now permanently settled. I really belonged in their home and I loved it." Her story includes tales of going to school, picnics and watching the circus parades.

It tells about meeting and marrying John, the arrival of their children and the succession of their work and homes.

This priceless story along with the genealogy that was collected from various relatives has been photocopied and distributed to family members. My grandchildren take "The Book" to school for Show and Tell and while some of them are more interested than others, the story is there when it becomes important for them.

My sister-in-law created **a beautiful family cookbook** that included old family photographs and charming family stories. She contacted all family members and invited them to ask their friends and other relatives to share their favorite recipes in *Jennie's Cookbook*. This work of "heart" features a hand-tinted childhood photograph of her mother, Jennie, pictured with her brother and sister. Printed by a cookbook publisher, this attractive collection of tried and true recipes is a treasure for the family.

Videotapes and audiotapes are another form of preserving family history. A friend said her family made a video of their parents' farmstead when we were sorting and dividing their estate. Ruby M. told about her large family reunion several years ago. The committee scheduled a bus to take the group on a York County tour to the homes where the families had lived as well as the home church, cemetery and other memorable sites. Recently, the family had a large reunion again in York County. This year the eldest living relative went on the same route and his daughter videoed the scenes they had toured before. Later they put this together with narration and made keepsake copies for all the family members.

Nearly twenty years ago, my mother moved to a nursing home in Lincoln to be near me. I worked full-time at the University and it was convenient for Mom to come to my home on Saturdays. She sat in her wheel-chair across the kitchen table from me. As we drank coffee she told her life story into a tape recorder. At first she was reluctant, but our talks stirred her memories. During the week she reflected on the events and situations of her growing years and she began to look forward to our Saturday storytelling sessions. Now, the sound of her voice on the cassette tapes is as precious as her stories.

Our grandkids also have histories and it's fun to record their little voices and childish words and antics. Long-distance grandparents can especially appreciate seeing videos and listening to audiotapes of young children. When I listen to the audiotapes of the grandchildren when they were small, the most irresistible ones are when the kids were acting up and not doing what I really wanted them to do. Hearing Emilie's made-up silly songs after she warbled through "I Saw Mommy Kissing Santa Claus" helps me recall that her creativity started early on.

Family reunions uncover talents that also make us proud of our relatives. For years we have enjoyed Cousin Evelyn's annual Christmas chronological poem, but we didn't know until last year that she could play the accordion. At the family reunion we also learned that Thelma's son works for a Congressman in Washington, D.C., and Maxine's grandson is entering the ministry. We saw photographs of the log cabin in the mountains of Colorado that Alyce and Vern built with their own hands.

"Family" and "reunion" go together like "sugar and spice," "bacon and eggs," "red, white and blue." If you have made it this far in *The Joy of Grandparenting*, you know the value of families getting together. My grandchildren learn history lessons by hearing how our pioneer grandparents built the homestead before South Dakota was a state, or the struggles on the farm during the Dirty Thirties or about Cousin Norman's work at Ames Laboratory in the development of the first atomic explosion.

Much has been written about family reunions.Here are a few suggestions to help you plan your own family gathering. In *A Better Tomorrow* Kathy Peel gives tips for organizing a reunion.

1) Divide the jobs and responsibilities with others and multiply the ideas and fun. This is good for small family get-togethers, too. Individuals take more interest when they have responsibilities...they take ownership in the event and want it to be successful.

2) Think about a reunion theme — celebrate your grandparents' anniversary, focus on your ethnic background.

3) Settle on a date as early as possible so it can be on your relatives' calendars.

4) Determine the location for the reunion. Consider places with motels, city and state parks and camping facilities.

5) Decide on details of date, location and expected cost and send a letter to all relatives asking them to send copies to others whose addresses you may not have.

6) Have your favorite "historian" organize an updated family tree. Ask family members to provide needed information and plan for its distribution.

7) Consider a potluck supper that includes the family's favorite foods: Aunt Minnie's fried chicken, Gladys's crystal salad, Violet's ham loaf, Aunt 'Manda's angel food cake, Earl's rhubarb delight. Since our last reunion was in the family's hometown, we expanded our last meal — a potluck — to include "shirt-tail-relatives."

8) Assign people to take on different jobs such as the talent show, sporting contests, memorabilia coordinator, tour leader. Our family has a watermelon-seed-spitting contest which is preceded, of course, with a watermelon feed. Horseshoes play a big part, but the main event is the Carlson Cousins' Golf Tournament complete with a trophy made of a two-by-four with a half-a-golf ball glued in the center.

9) Send a confirmation letter with all the important information.

10) Have nametags for each family member. Nametags can be organized according to family groups. An old picture of the original family members can be photocopied, separated, pasted to three-by-five cards and made for each attendee.

Plan for all ages at the reunion. Arrange for children's food to be available and plan simple craft activities or games that kids enjoy. Motels with pools and/or recreation facilities are great places for kids to hang out and get reacquainted while the old folks talk. State parks and camps work well for families. Consider that elders have comfortable seating and can participate in at least some of the family Olympics.

Cousin Kelley created more than 40 Carlson Reunion T-shirts. To our delight, Kelley designed a shirt with a slice of watermelon on a background of a blue and yellow Swedish flag. A picture of Kelley wearing the shirt along with an order blank was sent with one of the first informational letters. The shirts were distributed at the reunion.

Have a display of the family tree; use a large sheet of newsprint, a paper tablecloth, or a flattened refrigerator box. Two Carlson great-great-great-granddaughters, Stacey and Claire spent an afternoon recreating the fam-

Brothers Loren and Keith show off their Carlson colors.

ily tree on a blackboard. A friend has the family records on a large piece of oilcloth that can be rolled up and easily stored from one reunion to another.

Gather favorite recipes and put these together for distribution at a later time. Have family members bring vintage clothing for a style show. Encourage everyone to participate in a crazy hat parade. Give prizes for the craziest hat, the oldest hat, the one most like Grandma's, the prettiest, the most modern. Ask everyone to bring family photos and albums.

Ask the oldest family members to talk about the biggest changes they've seen, tell their happiest memories. Video portions of the reunion to share with relatives who are ill or oldsters who are unable to come. Send a greeting card signed by all the family members to absentees. Celebrate the birthdays nearest the date of the reunion.

Give awards at the end of the gathering; the traditional recognition of the oldest, the youngest, those who traveled the farthest. Include some silly prizes for the Worst Joke-Teller, the Mashed Potato Champion, the Best Napper, the Most Long-Winded. A computer-generated paper certificate is an inexpensive trophy. Elect officers to plan the next reunions.

There are many unique ways of celebrating kinship through reunions. Involving many relatives shares the responsibility and allows ideas to flow freely. Since books and other materials are available to guide you through reunion planning, I hope this limited discussion will "whet your appetite" for more.

Counselor friend Elinor reminds me that not everyone looks forward to family reunions. **Getting together after a time interval confronts us with losses.** Elders may have died and other relatives may be chronically or terminally ill. As we look around we see more pounds, more gray hair and more wrinkles that make us sad. Seeing certain family members may bring up painful memories. Sibling rivalry may be renewed although siblings usually grow closer in their later years.

How do we handle these situations? Elinor says it's important to realize that we always have choices. We don't have to stay stuck in the same situation we have always found ourselves. If we can not forgive and let go of the pain, we can at least resolve to understand ourselves and the others involved. We may want to seek professional help. The bottom line is how we want the next generation to remember us.

Dividing the family treasures is another process that often brings feelings to the fore. I remember listening to my folks talk about people who fought over their parents' estate and belongings after the funeral. They couldn't understand how property and things could be more important than relationships. I'm grateful for that lesson.

When my mother moved into a tiny retirement apartment, my brothers and I helped her prepare for an auction sale. We selected some of the antiques, heirlooms and treasures we wanted to keep in the family. In order to portion belongings equitably, we four children separated the things into groups of four of like classifications. For example, there were four groups of glassware and four heirlooms of similar value. For group one, Loren, the oldest had first choice and Paul, the second oldest, had second choice, etc. For group two, Paul had first choice and so on. Everyone had a first choice and everyone had last choice. We agreed that after the choices were made, we could trade with a sibling, though I don't know that any trading occurred.

The best thing that happened during this sharing of the family "jewels" was that Mom was there. As we made our choices, she reminded us of how that item came to be in the family. She said that the old copper teakettle, I wanted so badly and got on a third choice, came on the boat from Sweden. One of my pretty dishes was their wedding present from the Furlands — where Mom boarded while she was teaching school. We learned about our treasures and Mom had the satisfaction of knowing whose home it would be in.

Other families make variations of this procedure. If you cannot be together, you can take photos and distribute the "voting choices" by mail. You may feel slighted that your sister got the silver teapot you had always wanted. However, consider if having a sister is more valuable than the teapot.

Some elders give away their treasures to family members as wedding gifts, birthday presents or Christmas gifts. These gifts are even more meaningful when accompanied with notes explaining their significance to the family.

Grandparents are the hub of the family and the values, traditions, genealogy and family history are best explained by the elders in the family. Grandparents have the responsibility to carry on these important tasks as KINKEEPERS.

References for Genealogical Research*

1. *Fundamentals of Genealogical Research* by Laureen R. Jaussi and Gloria D. Chaston. 1977 (Deseret Book Co. Salt Lake City, Utah).
2. Military Service Records (NNCC) Washington, D.C. 20408. Write for the latest forms and price list.
3. *The Family Saga and Other Phases of Folklore.* A chapter on "The Family Saga as a form of Folklore" by Mody C. Boatright. Urbana: U. of Illinois Press. 1958.
4. Subscribe to *The Genealogical Helper* magazine from Everton Publishers, Inc., P.O. Box 368, Logan, Utah 84321. Or go to your State Historical Society and read their copies.

* This basic list of references was compiled by Marge Young.

Grandparents Are Bridgebuilders

*We may not always see eye to eye,
but we can try to see heart to heart.*
— from *More Heart Warmers,*
compiled by Helen Lesman

Grandparents are BRIDGEBUILDERS, bridging gaps of the generations, distance, divorce, desertion and drug addiction. We are the bridge from the past to the future. We provide continuity in our grandchild's generational legacy. The stories of our family life are living history. But the stories are more, they are the emotional and psychological heritage of family relationships. Ruth Goode says "it is no wonder that grandparents and grandchildren get along so well — they have a common enemy (the middle generation)... we and our grandchildren have the same target for our displeasure."

Dr. Arthur Kornhaber says that grandparents and grandchildren have a natural alliance of their own that may put them at odds with the middle generation. Generations that follow after one another often find deep-seated conflict, but amazingly, according to Kornhaber, that conflict is absent between the first and third generations. Perhaps the first and third generations get along better because neither had any choice in the relationship. "In both cases, it is something that happens to them, a gift. For children, it is the gift of life. For grandparents, it is a gift of a new connection" according to Kornhaber.

Our grandchildren hear complaints from their parents about us as their parents when they are growing up. "Your grandma used to..." or even now, "I wish Grandma would" are comments we don't often hear. There are times when we can admit to a grandchild that we wished we had handled a family situation differently. And when we hear the echoes of our own parenthood problems in the family of our adult child, we can look back with some detachment and at least share some understanding of the tough times our children face. The mature grandparent can be the bridge to understanding that makes the connection between the generations easier and smoother for all involved.

Sometimes we expect too much of our grandchildren and they can be painfully frank. I like the story of the little girl who snuggled up to her grandmother on the couch asking, "Guess who is my most favorite person in the whole wide world?" Grandmother gave her granddaughter an extra hug and purred, "I don't know, darling, who?" The little girl blurted out, "My other grandma."

Frances Weaver's granddaughter was tagging along behind her one busy morning. "What're you doin', Grandma?" "I'm straightening the living room. The girls are coming for bridge this afternoon." "What girls, Grandma?" By now the kid was jumping on the couch. "You know, Sarah. The girls I play bridge with on Wednesdays. My friends...." "Yeah, yeah, I know!" she crowed. "You mean the girls with the grandmother faces." Weaver recognized a good book title and so *The*

Girls with the Grandmother Faces became the title for her book on growing older with vim and vigor.

Lois Wyse, in *Funny, You Don't Look Like A Grandmother*, wrote about a friend whose grandson, feeling anxious about his new college roommates, called her to talk. The grandson explained one new friend hated his father, hoped he'd die and make him rich. Another roommate confessed he was gay. The grandson said, "Listen, Grandma. I'm not so sure I like this school. Around here nobody's like us."

The grandmother hoped she convinced her grandson to show compassion for his new friends but she understood the comfort her grandson wanted in talking with people like "us." She was grateful her grandson felt free to call her. She hoped her years of living helped her communicate with her grandson, perhaps even better than his parents. She said, "We (grandparents) got a lot of practice raising their parents."

Good communication is important for strong families. That can be difficult these days when the family is scattered all over the world and many grandparents are still involved in their careers with time constraints of their own. How can Grandma be there when the new baby arrives if she's defending a court case? What will your grandchildren know of "over the river and through the wood" if you live in a high-rise condo? When you're invited to Grandparents' Day, how do you explain you have airline tickets to go snorkeling in the Bahamas? We know our grandchildren have different lives than our own children, but we sometimes forget that grandparents are different, too. Our adult children, too, are often unaware of how times have changed.

We had pampered and petted our first grandchild for two years and then he moved with his Air Force father and mother 1500 miles away. We wondered if he would remember who we were and know that we loved him. How could we have any joy of grandparenting long distance?

That was the beginning of my academic study of grandparenting. My research of 270 grandparents was comforting. I learned that emotional closeness is proportional to the degree of contact. This should be no surprise; it is obvious that we have to know one another to have feelings for each other. The survey defined "contact" as a personal visit, a telephone call, or a letter or

"Can I talk to Grandma?
Can I talk to Grandma?
Can I talk to Grandma?"

REPRINTED WITH PERMISSION OF
BIL KEANE, GRANDFATHER OF 8.

package received by the grandchild. The research also showed that there must be some contact every two weeks for there to be a close emotional relationship.

Alexander Graham Bell must have been a grandfather who wanted to talk to his grandchildren when he invented the telephone. Talk to the little ones, even the babies. Their parents will tell you the little one's eyes light up and soon learn to recognize your voice. Be sure your grandchildren have pictures of you for their very own—ones they can hold or carry around in their play (the soft fabric frames are good choices). Perhaps you can attach a magnet and the picture can be "parked" on the refrigerator. Have your picture taken with a telephone in your hand so the child connects the voice on the telephone with your picture.

A little girl told her grandmother on the telephone that she had learned to turn a somersault. She said, "Watch me, Grandma." The mother said the toddler carefully placed the telephone receiver on the floor; promptly executed her best somersault and returned to the phone to listen for her grandmother's words of praise. A grandparent can help build self-esteem at a critical time with a phone call. After Grandpa had called specifically to talk to him, Markie crowed to his parents, "And, Grandpa didn't even mention math!"

The little boy in a *Readers' Digest* anecdote didn't recognize his grandfather's voice on the telephone. The grandfather called his daughter and her family who live over 1000 miles away. His four-year-old grandson answered, "This is Peter." Grandfather assumed his grandson would know his voice and asked, "Well, Peter, have you been a good boy today?" Peter replied, "Yup!" Grandfather continued, "Are you sure?" Peter said "Yup!" At this point grandfather asked if he could talk to the boy's mother. Peter called his mother to the phone and added, "I think it's the police."

Grandma Millie answered the phone and heard her tiny fifteen-month-old grandson's voice. He didn't talk much, but Millie continued her usual conversation with her grandson, asking about his activities. Soon her son-in-law came to the phone and asked who David was talking to. It seems the toddler had been playing with the phone and had pressed the automatic dialing button which made the connection to Grandma. You can't tell Grandma Millie that her grandson isn't more precocious than most.

Memory dialing systems and answering machines save precious minutes and make it easier for both the caller and the one who is called. When listening to the messages on my answering machine, I always get a flush of joy when I hear "I love you lots." Personal 800-numbers also are a wonderful invention. For a grandparent who wants to encourage telephone communication, contact your local telephone company for more information about 800-numbers.

Writing letters is as important now as it ever was. A love note addressed to your grandchild and delivered by the postal person is sure to make a hit. You don't have to buy expensive paper or notecards; use scraps of gift wrapping paper (leftover from the presents you sent) cut into squares and folded over to look like stationery. In a couple of short sentences with a bright colored felt tip pen tell your grandchild that you love him or her. My letters usually end with ❤ X ❤ X ❤ X. Draw a simple caricature of yourself for your signature. Mine is a smiley face with fuzzy hair on top and round blank eyeglasses. As a toddler Grandson Phillip loved getting his very own letters at his California home. His mother told me he carried them in his pocket, hauled them in his trucks and stashed them in his toy chest until they were tattered and torn. When talking to him on the phone, he mimicked my love notes saying, "I love you. Here's some hugs and kisses."

When writing to an older child, cut the letter into four or five parts like a puzzle. My only problem was that Markie's return letter was also cut into puzzle pieces — about fifty slivers. Construction paper or oaktag in colors works well for puzzles. Grandma Elizabeth reminded me that specialty stores and catalogs sell precut puzzles, ready to write on. Then you break up the puzzle and mail it in a special envelope provided with the purchase. These may be expensive, but are nice for a special occasion. Use interesting stamps on your letters. Commemorative stamps cost no more and you may introduce a grandchild to a lifelong hobby.

Have a good time creating a rebus for your message. That's when you draw an eye for the letter "I" or draw or cut out a picture of a hand for the word "hand" in your message. Kids love stickers and there are many choices in our stores for this inexpensive fun. One time, Elizabeth's grandson stuck the stickers all over her letter before it was read to him.

Grandpa Lou and Grandma Elizabeth have fun keeping in touch through the postal service with their grandsons Iain and Peter who were born and live in England. When the "Post" arrives at their London suburban home, three-year-old Iain knows the fuschia pink letters are his and eighteen-month-old Peter's letters are stop-sign yellow. In one letter, Grandpa Lou told Iain about his childhood country school experience with baby chicks hatching in an incubator. Grandpa asked if there were baby chicks at Iain's school. Later, Lou's telephone answering machine had Iain's answer, "No chickens, just teachers and children."

There were two dinosaur stickers on one letter Lou and Elizabeth received from England. Lou soaked the envelope in warm water and slid the stickers off onto the bright fuschia stationery. Grandpa Lou then drew cartoon bubbles over the dinosaur's heads as if the dinos were talking and telling Iain and Peter about their trip to America, their bath in the kitchen sink and subsequent return to England and Iain's "Post" box.

Marge and her four sisters have kept in touch with a round robin letter for many years. Three young women had so much fun hearing their mothers and mothers-in-law read their letters they have joined the letter writing troupe. Once in awhile the grandchildren even contribute. What a joyful day each sister has when the letters arrive!

Grandparents also find the cassette tape recorder/player is an excellent way to communicate with grandchildren. Having received the letters from Lou and Elizabeth, their daughter, Kristi, "talks" the letter to the children while the tape recorder is going. Grandma and Grandpa hear the children respond to their questions and they can listen to the tapes over and over. Sometimes Lou and Elizabeth play the tape several times to clearly understand Iain's and Peter's strong British accents.

Have your rebates or refunds sent directly to your grandchild. Your youngster will be excited about getting his own check. Cody lives near his Grandma. She gathers the materials and lets him send the rebates in. This keeps him out of his mother's hair and gives him experience in addressing and mailing letters.

Send postcards to your grandkids when you travel. You can keep postage for cards in your billfold. For extended travel, take along a set of preaddressed labels. (Remember, I have ten grandchildren!) The names remaining on my set remind me that I haven't written to them. Postcards are an inexpensive souvenir appropriate for any age. Small children like to see the animals of the area you are visiting and sports-minded teens enjoy seeing the sports arenas of the locality. Personalize the landmark postcards with an X to mark the spot where you stood. One grown man kept the postcards his grandmother sent when he was a young boy.

On occasions other than Christmas, Easter, Valentine's Day, or birthdays, send an *unbirthday* memento. Or make up a holiday, such as "Be Kind to Alex Day," or "God Bless Kory Extra-Good Day."

I don't write thank yous as often as I should, but there's no doubt **the best way to teach and encourage your grandchildren to write thank you notes is by example.** Thank them for the gifts, the time or visit they gave you. It doesn't always happen, but when you write, the children will write back. Sometimes, a self-addressed stamped envelope helps get a response. You can enclose a note on which the child can put a check mark beside the favored response, much like a school paper. Try to be cute or imaginative in putting the words together to make them think — and smile — at your efforts. Surely we can view these communications addressed directly to a specific grandchild as teaching courteous behavior, as well as whetting the child's appetite for reading and writing.

As I discussed in the chapter on magicians, another postal service that can enrich the grandparent/grandchild vital connection is a magazine subscription. *National Geographic World, Your Big Backyard, Highlights for Children, Ranger Rick* and *Sesame Street* are excellent publications for kids. Magazines that arrive in the mailbox can be a regular reminder of love to your grandchild.

The fax machine is a faster method of communication these days although our family hasn't yet taken that step. Grandpa Bud and Grandma Jackie helped each of their families have fax machines as Christmas presents last year. Much less expensive than a telephone call, a fax can reach people instantly. Grandma Christina received faxes from Ian and Catie the same day even though she was in Paris and they were in Boston. Legal documents and contracts under consideration can be viewed for family consultation adding practical value to a fax machine. Drawings, school papers and report cards can be shared with grandma and grandpa on the day of triumph. Another advantage is that you don't have to consider the time zones your children live in. A fax will not interrupt their dinner hour and the message will be there when they get home from school, piano lessons or karate classes.

Many of us olders are afraid of computers, modems and other technological paraphernalia, but we needn't be. Community colleges and senior centers all over the country offer computer classes at reasonable rates. If your grandchildren live near you, it's highly probable they can teach you how to use a computer. This will give your grandchild an extra boost of self-esteem and you will be more proud than he or she is.

Grandmother Luella was amazed that her four-year-old granddaughter used the computerized library checkout. I have learned to reset the clock in my car and change the time on my microwave from my grandchildren. Seeing six-year-old Alex program their VCR like a professional, made me follow instructions and learn to do it myself! I don't intend to be a fuddy-duddy old grandma that can't cope with change.

Grandparents are the "central news bureau" for the whole family, Ruth Goode says. Her suggestion inspired me to start our own postal service version of a family reunion — our family newsletter, "Dear Ones."

At the time my children were all over the world each doing their own thing. Cheryle was working in Washington, D.C., Becky was teaching in Australia, John was in the Air Force in California, North Dakota and later, Thailand and Korea, while Cyndi was living and working fifty miles away. My mother, the children's grandmother, had moved to a Lincoln nursing home. Going to college while working at the University full-time, I realized our family needed a communication system! "Dear Ones" provided critical information when Mom was dying and kept everyone informed—including my three brothers who lived in three other states. There was no other way I could have written that many individual letters. The time constraints of writing the weekly newsletter during my noon lunch hour forced me to keep the letter to one page, giving only the facts.

That was twenty years ago. "Dear Ones" format has changed somewhat and now is "published" monthly. However, the benefits read like Dave Letterman's:

Top Ten List of Reasons
To Write a Family Newsletter

10. You write one letter and print them out on your word processor or make photocopies for each of your adult children's families. Kids in college or working, get their own copies. If you don't type, your own handwriting with a dark felt-tip pen makes your letters even more personal and appealing. A writer friend's processor is her most wonderful letter-writing tool. She personalizes the beginning and the ending using the same body.

9. Everyone gets the same news at the same time — no complaints that someone didn't know what happened.

8. You can reread a letter but you can't reread a phone call.

7. Newsletters are short, concise and easy to read on-the-go, which most families are. Writing a letter allows you to more carefully phrase your words and allows readers to more thoughtfully consider their response.

6. Duplicate on the copy machine your last set of snap-shots along with the copies of your letter.

5. Your children are encouraged to contact you. They soon realize they won't rate much copy space if they haven't kept in touch. (Sometimes I call the kids to get a family update.)

4. You can give headlines for new or lost teeth, good grades, new jobs. All of us like to see our name in headlines, even my TV newsman son-in-law.

3. You can sneak in a little advice with an appropriate Ann Landers clipping, or a "Quote of the Week" that gives a message.

2. The letter is your journal or Instant Family History. Keep a copy of the letter for yourself. My fat note-books of previous Dear Ones collect dust now that a computer disk is reserved for Dear Ones.

And the number one reason to send a family newsletter is:

1. It's easier to say "I LOVE YOU" in a letter.

♥x♥x♥x♥x♥x♥x♥x♥x♥

Of course, you have to be fair and diplomatic since everyone is going to read the same letter. You don't want to make too big a deal about Baby Sara's first steps unless you will do the same when her cousin Sophie begins to walk. I have even counted the number of lines for each family in my effort to be equitable. Grandparents should try to be nonpartisan.

I used to brag about "Dear Ones" being a "good news only" letter, but I have changed my mind. Other grandparents agree that a family needs to share the bad news, too, so we can be a support network for one another. You should be able to tell your troubles to your family.

Besides the updates on the family, include news from where you live — the rebuilding progress of the court house that burned; the visit to the county fair or a movie mixed with memories of the olden days. Ask their opinion about what kind of car to buy or their thoughts on national politics.

Safety is the most important factor when you welcome your grandchildren into your home. Don't forget about the dangers of pills, medications lined up on your bathroom and kitchen counters. Cover electrical outlets. Keep electrical cords out of the way. Be sure to turn handles for cooking pans away from the stove front. Keep knives and scissors put away when not in use. If it's unsafe to bring the toddlers and small babies to grandmother's, the young family will not come to visit. If Jill is eight months old when she visits, plan for a bed or playpen and an arrangement for feeding her. Discuss this with her parents before they arrive. They may bring a portable crib or a stroller (which can double as a feeding station). When my neighbors meet their grandchildren at the plane, they take two cars to manage all the baby equipment. Cribs and other equipment also can be borrowed from friends or rented.

Grandmother Joan M. has a fully equipped nursery for her grandbabies — including disposable diapers, an extra baby bottle, pacifier and several teddy bears. Grandma Kay has a bedroom reserved for her grandchildren when they sleep over. When I moved to a different house, I waited until my grandkids came to visit to put "their room" in order. They helped make the beds and decided where their things would be. Use an old plastic tablecloth to protect a mattress on an adult bed for a temporary situation.

If the children are small, be sure to put your keepsakes, figurines and antiques away so you don't have to be watching and saying "no, no" all the time. Plastic plugs can be purchased economically to insert in electrical outlets to safeguard the babies who are creepers and crawlers. Your adult children will appreciate your consideration and visit often.

Of course, you will plan your menus to include the favorite foods of your adult children as well as your grandchildren. Grandmothers can teach table manners and conversation by setting a pretty table and encouraging the niceties of dining. Seeing a *Good Housekeeping* article entitled "Family Dinners: Time for Conversation" made me realize how much families have changed. The article suggested l) make dinner an event to celebrate, 2) begin the meal with a ritual—a prayer, holding hands, a toast, or each person's review of the day, 3) watch your words, 4) don't moralize 5) don't expect the experience to be perfect. Most grandparents of today accepted family dinners and conversation of their day as the "only way to do things." Some of us are astonished these things need to be taught.

When Carrie and her three girlfriends stayed overnight at my house following a teen concert, I surprised them with a "ladies brunch" the next morning. We ate in the dining room with nice dishes, napkins and a centerpiece. We had fruit slush served in sherbet dishes, a breakfast casserole and gooey cinnamon rolls, The girls drank their milk from crystal goblets acting very mannerly.

Bridging the gap between her grandchildren, their stepfather and their birth father has been a challenge for my friend. Marge has been widowed twice and lost a daughter to cancer. She spent several weeks with her daughter as she fought her illness, leaving seventeen-year-old Laura and fourteen-year-old Shawn. The children lived with their stepfather until he remarried. Laura went on to college and Shawn moved to live with his paternal grandmother (his birth father's mother).

Marge was a lifeline to Laura as she struggled to work while finishing college in three years. Her grandmother sent "care packages," car repair funds, a roll of quarters for the laundramat and helped her shop for an interview outfit. Laura knew she could telephone her grandmother collect any time about anything. Recently, Laura called to tell her grandmother that her dream job has become a reality. Most of all, Laura cherishes her grandmother's thoughtfulness and her prayers. She said, "Grandmother, you are the only reason I made it."

"I feel I've really been a bridgebuilder," Grandma Esther said. Her son and daughter-in-law were divorced when their two daughters were very young. But Esther did not let that spoil her relationship with her grand-daughters in their blended family. Her granddaughter, Laura, a college student, asked if she could stay with Esther while she has a summer job in Lincoln. Esther didn't take long to consider, "Won't that be wonderful, to have her coming and going all summer long?" One of Laura's friends asked Esther if she would insist on a curfew. "Heaven's no. She's twenty years old."

Grandparent bridgebuilders are mediators. Grandma Eva has learned that grandchildren don't have to be very old before they start negotiating. At three-and-a-half, Chuckie found his social life at preschool interrupted when his mother stayed home with him and his new baby brother Drew. Chuckie and his mother visited a near-by preschool that was very attractive but the school required all children must be toilet-trained. Since Drew's arrival, Chuckie had regressed, but he assured his daddy that he could meet the regulations since it was quite a while before preschool started. Chuckie said, "I can poop in my pants until school starts." But Dad said, "No way. You must cooperate now."

That's when Chuckie got on the phone and called Grandma 200 miles away. Eva listened while Chuckie told his story and then asked Eva to please tell his parents that he should be allowed to go to preschool no matter what. Grandma Eva reminded him that baby Drew couldn't go to preschool because he couldn't use the toilet and she agreed with his parents. Then, Chuckie said, "Grandma, I thought you'd be on my side."

♥x♥x♥x♥x♥x♥x♥x♥x♥x♥

**If Mommy says no, ask Grandma.
Grandparents "no" better.**

♥x♥x♥x♥x♥x♥x♥x♥x♥x♥

Five-year-old Alex apparently shares the perception that grandparents are bridgebuilders. Recently while he was with Grandma Luella, he said, "My dad is mean." Luella said, "Really? Why do you say that, Alex?" He explained, "Well, he won't let me have a dog." He thought a moment and then continued. "Grandma," he said, "You're his mother. You should tell him to get me a dog. Every kid needs a dog." Grandma Luella wasn't quite sure this sort of bridgebuilding was part of her grandma job description.

I found myself in the middle of a parent-grandson situation, too. When I asked Mark what he wanted for his seventeenth birthday. He said, "Grandma, all I want is peace in our world, a beautiful girl to love me, a flashy new car and a tattoo." My response was, "OK, I can handle that." Then, over the phone I heard Mark holler, "Dad, Grandma says I can have a tattoo." Not thinking any more of his remark, I planned my clever retort. Manufacturing my own card; on the first page I drew a globe and wrote PEACE on top. Next was a picture of myself and my affirmation that I was the "pretty girl who would always love" him. A classy red sports car was cut from a magazine and Garfield stickers were my symbol of a tattoo.

Sightseeing with Mark in Salzburg.

Several years later while visiting Mark at his army base in Germany, he reminded me of that birthday wish and showed me a tattooed bracelet on his upper arm. Not knowing what to say, a great-uncle who was a tattooed man in the circus seventy-five years ago came to mind. I told Mark that Great-Uncle J. was not only known for his tattoos but for his strong leadership with the Gideon Bible Society and the Methodist Episcopal Church. (That's the truth!) What do you think, was I straddling the fence or was I a bridgebuilder?

There are many kinds of bridges — quaint bridges over fake gravel pools, sturdy concrete bridges over irrigation ditches and the huge spans of cables and steel over harbor inlets. Whatever the need or reason, grandparents can be BRIDGEBUILDERS.

♥X♥X♥X♥X♥X♥X♥X♥X♥

The Bridgebuilder

An old man going a lone highway
Came in the evening cold and gray
To a chasm vast and deep and wide.
The old man crossed in the twilight dim,
The sullen stream had no fears for him,
But he stopped when safe on the other side
And built a bridge to span the tide.
"Old man," said a fellow pilgrim near,
You are wasting your strength with building here;
Your journey will end with the ending day,
You never again will pass this way.
You've crossed the chasm deep and wide,
Why build you this bridge at evening tide?"
The builder lifted his old gray head.
"Good friend, in the path I have come," he said,
"There followeth after me today
A youth whose feet must pass this way.
This chasm which has been a naught to me
To that fair-haired youth might a pitfall be.
He, too, must cross in the twilight dim. Good friend,
I am building the bridge for him."
                          Will Allen Dromglow

(John Orr used this poem at many 4-H events.)

♥X♥X♥X♥X♥X♥X♥X♥X♥

Grandparents Are Heroes

*If you want to know how to live your life, think
about what you would like people to say about you
after you die, then live backwards.*
— Michael Josephson

One of the most awesome responsibilities and most wonderful opportunities grandparents have is that of HERO or role model. We don't talk a lot these days of heroes and heroines but most of us grandparents think in these terms even though our grandchildren may not. We remember reading about Horatio Alger, the legendary poor boy who was successful in everything he did because he demonstrated all the virtues of good character — especially persistence and hard work. Horatio Alger showed us that character is what we all need to fall back on when things are tough.

In these times, Fred Rogers, of Public Broadcasting, has been teaching values to young children through the television show, "Mr. Rogers' Neighborhood" for twenty-five years. Someone said that he may have touched more lives than anyone else in the world.

However, many of our grandchildren think more of the superheroes of the times — the Teenage Mutant

Ninja Turtles, Superman and Spiderman, who are successful in battling crime and evil only because they have supernatural powers. We grandparents worry when we think of some of the TV comics that model violence such as Power Rangers and Beavis and Butthead.

When calling up my computer thesaurus, I was shocked to find "hero" defined as "a famous person" and synonymous with "celebrity." What happened to the idea that heroes were heroic? My thoughts went to celebrities — Michael Jackson, O.J. Simpson, Jim Baker and Pete Rose — who have fallen off their hero pedestals.

Irving Rein, Northwestern University professor, says the ancient Greeks believed "a hero had to be a maker of speeches and a doer of deeds." But our definition changed in the '20s and '30s when the media began to promote and develop celebrity and star status. According to Jack Christe of Ripon College if we want real heroes, we must give up celebrity worship. "A real hero invests extraordinary effort in achieving a goal on behalf of other people," That better fits my definition of grandparents as heroes.

I was also relieved to find my kind of definition when I went to my Merriam Webster's Collegiate Dictionary. There was nothing about celebrities, but 1) "one admired for his (or her) achievements and noble qualities," 2) "one that shows great courage," and 3) "an object of extreme admiration and devotion." This affirms my thoughts that many grandparents are heroes.

As he was driving with his grandson beside him, Granddad T.R. wasn't thinking about definitions of words. He thought he was answering the little boy's questions in pretty good shape until Steve threw him a ringer:

Grandson: Who first **used** words?
Granddad: Mmm...Mmmm...Mmm!

Grandson: Well, who first **made** words?
Granddad: Well, Mmmmmm...Mm...Mmm.
Grandson: Who first made BAD words?
Granddad: Well, I think Mmmm...Mmm...Mm!
Grandson: WHY DID THEY MAKE BAD WORDS?
Granddad: Well, we're home now wasn't that a
   nice ride?

❤x❤x❤x❤x❤x❤x❤x❤x❤

We wonder what impact we can have on the development of our grandchildren's values and character. How can we make a difference in the moral and ethical growth of our grandchildren? Talking with my grandparent friends, I hear their strong concerns about the prevalence of violence in our society. We talk about the violence on television and what we can do about it. At a recent gathering we heard a TV news director and a newspaper film critic explain the complexities of monitoring the media.

The news director said that we **can** make a difference if we make our complaints known to the right people. We do not have to feel helpless or victimized. As we are better informed and have more knowledge we know how to bring about change.

Eda LeShan says "What has not changed one iota is a role grandparents have had all along: to be on the side of what is absolutely right. Moral values and ethical human relationships remain our business. We are against people hurting each other."

We must be true to our values and stand up for what we believe is right. This is not the same as passing on our religious faith. Ethics is ethics, there is no distinction in the area of academic thought. Ethics applies to all religions, to all facets of life, to all occupations and careers. It applies to the way we live our lives.

In a SAGE class, (Sharing Across Generations for Enrichment) the University of Nebraska's Lifelong Learning Program, we have studied ethics and learned about the Josephson Institute of Ethics. It made me feel good to know that other grandparents have a sense of urgency to help their grandchildren know of values and virtues, goodness and morality. SAGE Director Deanna Eversoll explained it this way, "Ethics is not about the way things are, it is about the way things ought to be." My friends' daughter, Nancy Moser, says, "Characters live to be noticed, and people with character notice how they live."

We can help our grandkids learn about values clarification, motivation and planning for long term goals. Grandparents can influence character formation in many ways — how we act in private in their homes or in our homes, when we are together in public places or over distance through letters and telephone. We also influence their lives by not acting or when silent.

Don't be ashamed to teach values and virtues. Judge W. W. Nuernberger retired from the Juvenile Court bench some time ago. In their backyard, the Nuernbergers have a visual display of their code for living. On a piece of soft sandstone are carved the Ten Commandments as a constant reminder for all their family and friends.

The Josephson Institute provides another example of the difference grandparents can make. The ethical grandparent tells the family group there may not be much of a Christmas celebration since the grandparent took a stand against bribery and theft in the workplace and the loss of the family business is a grave threat. "I did it for you, my family," the ethical grandparent says.

On the other hand the unethical grandparent tells the family of plans for a wonderful Hawaiian holiday to include the extended family. It is also revealed that the vacation funds were obtained illegally. "But, I did it all for you, my family," the unethical grandparent says. Michael Josephson, the founder of the Institute says, "Even if you win the rat race, you're still a rat."

By sharing our experiences we can introduce our grandchildren to a variety of career possibilities. Grandson Patrick, 9, came along to visit my cousin Norman who was recovering from kidney surgery. These two special people needed to meet each other since they had common interests. A couple of years earlier, Patrick had told me he either wanted to be a professional baseball player, an auto mechanic or a nuclear physicist when he grows up. Norman was a retired nuclear physicist.

Over breakfast Norman talked about his career. He considered his greatest professional contribution to be the development of the zirconium alloy, a metal housing of plutonium on nuclear submarines. He and Patrick also had great fun sharing baseball trivia. Patrick perked up his ears when Norman confessed that he really wanted to be a professional baseball player. This little excursion took on more significance a few months later when Norman passed away. Although their acquaintance was short-lived, Patrick will remember Norman, the nuclear physicist and baseball-player-wanna-be.

Robert Butler, M.D., first director of the National Institute on Aging, says his relationship with his grandmother stimulated his early interest in aging. Butler was reared by a single mother who died when he was still young. Being raised by his grandmother prompted his life-long interest in older people.

Grandparents in politics can model examples of good citizenship for their grandchildren. Although he was an infant, the grandson of Nebraska's Governor Kay Orr, got a head start on knowing his place in the political world when he went to the National Republican Convention with his grandparents and parents and was photographed with Senator and Mrs. Jack Kemp. Taylor Christian will no doubt see those pictures and hear the story of his very early attendance in the political arena.

Grandparents like to think they may have something to do with their grandchildren's success. At least, that's how I felt when my daughter-in-law went on about my grandson's achievement in his new bank position. She said his caring attitude toward his elderly clients was one of his best attributes. On his day off, John went to the bank in his golf togs, specifically to meet an older woman who had a certificate of deposit coming due that day. I can't claim I gave John banking lessons or lectured him on being nice to old folks. But John has grown up knowing four grandparents who loved and cared for him. He knew them as examples of the aging population and transferred his personal responsibility to the older client.

I was invited to a Christmas musicale performed by two friends. The beautiful home was festive with two Steinway concert grands in the limelight of Marilyn's studio. Nine-year-old Brittany watched as her over-80-year-old Grandmother Pauline and her neighbor, Marilyn, played J. S. Bach and Christmas carols, as well as several jazz arrangements by Chip Davis of Mannheim Steamroller.

Brittany had flown alone from Texas to be with Pauline on this first Christmas since her husband's death. Grandmother and granddaughter each had practiced piano, read and played games filling the holidays. Brittany hardly realized her grandmother's remarkable abilities to overcome the trauma of the recent death of her husband of so many years, while she prepared for and performed the holiday concert so beautifully. In the life of her Grandmother Pauline, Brittany continues to see a wonderful example of faith and tenacity with enthusiasm for life after her losses.

Grandma Betty is a powerful example of positive aging. She spent her sixty-ninth birthday on a trailride in the Superstition Mountains. Frequently, she is the oldest person on trailrides in the area. A young neighbor, Melissa, was 14 or 15 when she started to ride with Betty. They have become fast friends as they travel around the Midwest pulling the horse trailer and keeping their gear together. Unpredictable weather sometimes keeps them in the close quarters of the pickup. Betty and Melissa treasure these times for reading and sharing thoughts and confidences.

Often this same ranch-bred grandmother leaves her city home and drives her pickup to the cabin near the ranch where her son and his family live. When her grandson was eight, Betty gave him one of the old traps she had used as a youngster. Jared quickly caught on to this new venture and proudly showed Grandma Betty his skunk and possum trophies on her next visit. Grandmothers and grandfathers come in a variety of packages, but they have to, to meet the needs of these diverse grandchildren.

We often forget how frequently we model behavior for our grandchildren. When grandma and mom went shopping, they left specific instructions for Grandpa Richard to take his young grandson to the bathroom. Not quite remembering how he handled the situation when his own sons were that age, Richard chose to demonstrate. When he had finished, the little tot clapped his hands and said, "Good job, Grandpa!" Grandpa Roger had the same responsibility with young Ryan. Roger helped the little boy with a troublesome zipper and then Ryan asked for privacy solemnly dismissing him, "You can leave now, Grandpa."

We are living examples of growing old. Children who have grown up in close relationships with their grandparents are oblivious to the negative aspects of aging. As I was holding my four-year-old granddaughter's hand, we each noticed the difference in our hands at the same time. Claire looked at me thoughtfully saying, "Someday, my hands will look just like yours." I sensed that she actually wanted her smooth, dimpled hands to have brown spots and bulging, blue veins.

A grandma friend who spends summers with her grandchildren at the lake said her seven-year-old grandson was worried about her until she explained that the varicose veins, so obvious when she wore a swim suit, were not a terrible malady or a fatal illness. Grandchildren do care and are concerned for their loving grandparents.

Grandparents often have to explain more serious health problems such as strokes, heart attacks, cancer and Alzheimers. Children have a way of understanding life and illness when they have positive connections with their grandparents. Seeing their grandparents age and watching their physical bodies and minds deteriorate helps children accept aging as part of the life cycle.

Grandma Gladys C.'s seven grandchildren watched her leukemia-like illness take it's toll for fifteen years. She and Grandpa Jim were in the same hospital at the same time when he had a heart valve replacement. Their 50th wedding anniversary was celebrated together even though the necessary oxygen precluded candles on the cake. As the grandchildren grew they saw their grandparents through several other health and medical crises.

The five girl cousins were in college and working, but they drove five and six hours to be with Grandma and Grandpa at their retirement home. The girls stayed at a motel, took their grandparents out to eat and went back to Wesley Acres Home to play games and cards. A week before she died, the girls had their reunion again although Gladys was hospitalized. A grandson, working in London, got the news of her death too late to come to the funeral. Instead, Chad flew to South Dakota the day after the funeral and stayed with his grandfather for the next few days.

Being close to their little Grandma Gladys (whose height had diminished six or seven inches in their lifetimes) did not make the funeral any easier for them. However, the tributes from her pastor and friends surely were comforting and made them proud.

When the grandchildren were small, Gladys and Jim went to great effort to have the family together for holidays and vacations. Gladys baked for weeks to prepare each grandchild's favorite food or treat. Sleeping bags were all over the farm house for days. Maybe there were hurt feelings once in awhile with the close quarters, but the reunions continued with regularity as the kids grew. The young adult grandchildren continue to come back to be with Grandpa Jim as often as they can. The long-term investment of spending time together is paying great dividends for all three generations.

When grandchildren are part of a loving, caring extended family, the chances are good they will have a positive attitude toward older people. However, the opposite is also true. When there is feuding and fighting around the extended family table, it is likely the children will respond the same way as they grow older.

I remember the poignant parable of an old grandfather who often spilled his food and was required by his son and daughter-in-law to eat out of a wooden bowl in a corner of the kitchen. One day their little boy was diligently carving when his mother asked what he was doing. He said he was making something just for her — a wooden bowl for her to eat out of when she was as old as grandfather. Children learn attitudes through their close relationships.

Dr. Arthur Kornhaber, who has worked with inner city delinquents and gang members, reports that kids who have a close relationship with their grandparents develop respect for elders and will rarely rob or hurt older persons (unless their minds are affected by drugs). Many delinquents do not mind embarrassing their fathers or mothers, but they do not want to bring shame to their grandparents.

When my oldest grandson was married, I wanted to give him and his new bride something symbolic of family. Since John and Tanya like traditional things, my gift was a counted cross-stitch wedding sampler. (After realizing the hours required, my wisdom in setting a precedent for the first of possibly ten grandchildren's weddings is questionable!)

The meaning of family took on special significance for me while cross-stitching. I recalled my own marriage and remembered a precious letter we had received from my husband's grandmother. The letter was in several safety deposit boxes through the years but miraculously it survived and said much of what I wanted tell John and Tanya. Part of her letter is below:

Dear Grandchildren,

Time has passed so swiftly since I last saw you. I didn't realize it had been so long. I am thinking of you just starting out on the long journey of life. It is all before you, and I am nearing the end. How well I remember when your grandfather and I began our life together, we were young, too. We made mistakes, but everything turned out all right. And those memories are precious.

With love and best wishes,
Grandmother

Recalling that cherished letter, reminded me of the blessing Grandmother had given us. I, too, wanted to pass on a blessing to this grandson, who carries his great-great-grandfather's name. With Victorian-like floral stationery I formed my thoughts to John and Tanya. Copying Grandmother's letter for myself and my children, I placed the original letter with my letter inside an envelope and attached it to the back of the framed wedding sampler. John and Tanya's reaction as they opened the gift made this grandmother realize all her efforts were not in vain. This was a very happy occasion.

When my daughter viewed her Grandma Jennie's wedding dress, I'm sure she remembered that lovely lady who was a perfect model of graciousness and good manners even in her tan plaid housedress. Although my daughter was small when her grandmother died, her beautiful memories were affirmed when she saw the lovely old gown.

Sometimes when our grandchildren look up to us it doesn't seem so serious. I'm thinking of the times my little granddaughters dressed up in old finery — hats, lacy slips, fancy aprons, crocheted shawls — they looked pretty silly tossing their heads, pursing their lips, mimicking my walk.

Eventually there comes the time when we have to look up to

Grandma hardly "measures up" to Phillip, 13.

the "little kids." We have a ritual of taking pictures of grandma with the grandchildren to measure how much the kids have grown. (Gratefully we document height and not weight!) It's kind of nice to be considered the yardstick, the standard or the benchmark of the family. The time is coming, very soon, that grandma will be the shortest one in the family. On the other hand, it's alarming and sometimes frightening to know that we grandparents have to measure up to our grandchildren.

Matthew, 16, built a remote controlled sailboat.

Grandson Matthew, 16, answered the phone so I asked, "Tell me what's going on in your life." All in one breath he replied, "Well, my teacher really likes my art project and wanted to put it on the front cover of all our designs, but there's rampant censorship by the old people on the school board so it won't get picked." Matt's words about the "rampant censorship by the old people on the school board" made my hackles stand up but I restrained my reaction with, "Tell me about your project."

"It's a linoleum print of a school desk duplicated several times. It's the statement underneath that says

'Exercise in Conformity' that they don't like. If I take the statement off, they'll use it." Defensive about the hackles and ready to lecture, I slowly reframed my thoughts, "What are you going to do, Matthew?"

It didn't take him long to answer, "I'm not going to take it off. I'm not going to compromise my values. That would destroy the integrity of my work."

Right on Matthew! How can you hug over the phone? Matt was way ahead of his grandmother. He said all the right words — "not compromise my values-the integrity of my work," that affirmed and validated my belief in my grandson's character. Later, I wonder if my willingness to listen to his story will make a difference in his sixteen-year-old attitude toward the "old people on the school board."

However, in that short conversation, Matthew taught me a valuable lesson — listen to the whole story before offering criticism or advice.

All grandparents are not HEROES, but even ordinary grandparents can make a difference living authentic lives based on strong character and high values.

Grandparents Are Beacons

We all know grandparents whose values
transcend passing fads and pressures, and who
possess the wisdom of distilled pain and joy.
— President Jimmy Carter

Grandparents are BEACONS or spiritual guides, a weighty, solemn role. Educator, writer and counselor Eda LeShan writes that she was a wonderfully lucky child with four grandparents to love her. "But that wasn't the whole story. They were also beacons of light in teaching me what it meant to be an ethical, moral, caring person. Their passionate sense of family was a bulwark against all the normal terrors of life," she said.

Some people, especially women, have difficulty relating to God as Father since their earthly fathers have not been good fathers. The Native American culture holds grandfathers in highest respect. Georgiana Sanchez suggests adopting the Native American tradition of relating to God as Heavenly Grandfather.

Many writers are aware of the spiritual bond between grandparents and grandchildren. Marilyn Morgan Helleberg wrote in a *Daily Guideposts* (1994) meditation, "Someone said that every newborn baby is a message from God that the world should go on." About her new little granddaughter, "God writes that message for the future all over my heart."

Writer Fay Angus repeated her rugged, hard-working, husband's reaction to their first grandson: "This little fellow has given me a whole new beginning...He has never seen me angry,...lose my temper...Never seen me slam a door with irritation...and I hope he never will!"

According to Wendy Wright, a Creighton University (Omaha, Nebraska) family life theologian, "The dynamics of our spirituality is made known through the God-moments of our family relationships." Her message affirms the response to grandparenting that so many of us have.

Comments about grandparenting from Tom Osborne, the nation's winningest football coach, and his wife Nancy clearly demonstrate a spiritual side to grandparenting. Grandmother Nancy said, "The birth of our first grandchild, Will, has rekindled our appreciation of little ones and the breath of fresh air they bring to our lives. Will reminds us to stop the clock...to take time to lay on our backs in the grass and imagine what cloud shapes are...to lose ourselves in awe of a ladybug or a caterpillar going about its daily business. After bringing into the world three precious ones of our own, we didn't know that we had the capacity for this kind of love again."

When thinking of my own grandparents who died many years ago, my foremost thought is that sense of spirituality that gives meaning and purpose to living. That presence has come from my parents, grandparents, forefathers and foremothers.

It becomes real to me in two ways. Their legacy of life has helped me know how to live...and how to die. And a religious heritage provides a foundation that underlies all I am. This spiritual legacy gives meaning and purpose to my life.

The issues of life and death are overwhelming for all of us and especially bewildering for children. Alex was three when his Grandma Pat died. He went along to Illinois making several trips with his parents while she was ill and later to take care of her belongings. One day Alex's mother, my daughter Becky, told him they were going to Grandma's. Alex asked, "Do you mean my dead grandma's or my live grandma's?" She told him they were coming to my house in Lincoln. But that confused Alex even more and he asked, "Well, then where does my dead Grandma live?"

Ramona Warren's devotional *Loving Legacy* includes a story taken from a "Dear Abby" column of a little girl's explanation of her grandmother's death. After the funeral, the little girl said, "Mom, you always said that Grandma walked and talked a lot with God." The little girl said she thought that one day God and Grandma went for an extra long walk, and walked so far, that God said to Grandma, "You are a long way from home and are so tired, you had better just come home with me and stay." The little girl added, "And Grandma went."

Most of us have tender moments with our grandchildren when we recognize that our grandchildren know we are "old." In their innocence, trusting our truthfulness and authenticity as elders, grandkids ask about moles, wrinkles, false teeth and varicose veins. One youngster, seeing her grandmother in a swimming suit, naively remarked, "Grandma, you sure jiggle a lot."

Michael was eight when I visited one holiday and was finishing an afghan for their family. He was bound and determined that he would learn how to crochet. It was a struggle for both of us. He didn't really learn much about crocheting, but at that visit, I think he learned about saying goodbye.

The night before I was to leave, after we'd finished our spaghetti dinner, Michael asked if he could pray again. So, we bowed our heads. I was especially touched when Michael prayed that "tomorrow, everyone in the whole wide world would be safe wherever they are."

Then, in the airport as we were saying our good-byes, a very sober Michael stood before me and said, "This is a very sad day in my life. It reminds me of the day my cat died."

I had heard that cat tale and it was indeed a sad memory. But I took his hands in mine and looked into his eyes and assured him that there was a difference. Although his cat had used up his proverbial nine lives and couldn't come back, I would be back. When I made that return visit one of the first things I did was to remind Michael that I had come back as I had promised.

Sally VanZandt, University of Nebraska-Lincoln gerontology researcher who studied the grandparent relationship from the perspective of college-age grandchildren, reports that 82 percent of the grandchildren said that their grandparents helped them find purpose and meaning in life and make them feel their life is important.

Ninety percent of the grandchildren relate that their grandparents have a positive impact on their lives and 70 percent want to have more contact with their grandparents.

With her failing health Granny Cope and her husband moved next door to a small no-basement house from their big family home across town. She had her own lending library of mostly "Little Golden Books" and encouraged the children in the neighborhood to borrow them if they copied the title and signed their names on the tablet in her living room. On hot summer days — before we had air conditioning — the children would gather around her under the big cottonwood tree on the corner of 60th and Judson and listen to her read stories. Bambi was one of the favorites.

In the fall Granny Cope spent the dimes she had saved for tulip bulbs to take the children to see the movie *Bambi* at the Joyo Theater. A couple of us mothers loaded all the kids into our cars; little David and his wheelchair went along. Granny also bought popcorn for our neighborhood crew. A few weeks later, she was in the hospital. When I went to see her, she knew she was dying and told me, "Tell the children that Granny is just going on another great adventure. And the worst thing is that I can't write and tell them all about it."

Granny Cope didn't need her dimes for spring bulbs that fall — she saw beautiful blooms in the faces of the happy children. She was a marvelous grandmother to the neighborhood children and a first-class grand-mother model for me. Not only did she show us how to live but also how to die.

A teen-age boy learned about dying from his grand-mother. Karen Henry Clark quoted his tribute to his grandmother at her funeral in *Reader's Digest*: "She put up an incredible fight to the end, when she died peace-fully, which is how she lived her life. That was Nana's way, and I hope I can carry on in the same manner."

Frequently the aging process has to be explained. In-terpreting and trying to help children understand about strokes, Alzheimers, cancer, heart attacks, major depression and death is very difficult and can be heart-wrenching. However, it is important that children be included in what is going on when a cherished grandparent is suffering. Not knowing what is happening causes more stress than to have an understanding of the problem.

At the age of eight, Annie was totally involved in the several crises and trauma of the passing of her great-grandmother. Regularly, Annie was with Great-Grand-mother Lois when she was in her own home, then her nursing home room, and she was there to say her final goodbye, caressing her hands and face in the hospital. Annie's sensitive and caring concern gave strength and courage to her grandparents and helped ease the pain for her parents and her little cousins.

The minister at Annie's great-grandmother's funeral was aware of the importance of involving the children in the mourning process. After the committal service at the graveside, he spoke directly to the children, although the adults appreciated his comments, too. He explained that their gentle, kind, Great-Grandmother Lois, who they fondly remembered baking cookies and giving them hugs, was not in the box with her worn-out body. She was in another world without pain and the children could hold her in their hearts and memories until they would be reunited.

Funerals can provide a wonderful rebonding time. Someone said that **funeral reunions are the last best gift that our dear ones give to us**. My brother Paul's funeral was the occasion for the rest of our family to be reunited. Paul and his family had moved to the East Coast when their children were small. We had been together infrequently, but this sad time with his wife Violet, children and grandchildren and my brothers, Loren and Keith was very special.

We adults talked long over our coffee cups. The grandkids poured out their feelings on pencil and paper writing stories about Pop-Pop Paul. Monica said "he had more patience than a lot of people." According to Kevin, "Pop-Pop always carved cool things." Philip wrote that Paul loved tractors and toothpicks. To Chrissa, Paul's Christmas organ concerts were "the sweetest sound I have ever heard." The older girls both remembered his humor and his insight: Adriane wished he were still living so she could get to know him better. Erika summed up all their feelings describing her grandfather as a quiet patriarch.

My brother's grandchildren told me lovely things about him I didn't know and their endearing recollections comforted me. The writing exercise helped the kids express their feelings and accept the reality of their grandfather's death. The kids also gained a sense of their own value as they remembered their good times together. For his grandchildren, Pop-Pop's memory will continue as a beacon or guiding light in their search for life's meaning.

Karen Henry Clark wrote, "When you say goodbye to a beloved grandparent, you say goodbye to something happy, something young in yourself, and that something never really returns, and the pain never really goes away."

Some of us never outgrow the need for a role model to help us know how to live and die. My mother at age 79 hadn't lived in a nursing home very long when she confided that she tried to be like Mrs. Butler who lived across the hall. Mrs. Butler was 101 years old and Mom admired her positive attitude and pleasant manner.

There's one job or task which is appropriate for all grandparents. We can always pray for our families, children and grandchildren. One time I asked my mother for help with a thorny problem...that doesn't seem important now. Sitting in her wheelchair with a crocheted afghan over her lap, she said, "I can't do much about it. But I can pray. And I will pray." Just knowing that my mother was praying for me lifted my burden. And life did get better.

At a Lenten Breakfast discussion a young adult friend, Dawn, championed the effects of prayer in our lives. "Whenever something bad is happening to me, I can hold on until Friday, 'cause that's the day my grandmother prays for me." She went on to relate that her grandmother has seven grandchildren and she prays especially for one each day.

Dawn's words prompted me to develop a prayer schedule for my own grandchildren. Since I have ten grandchildren I pray for two grandchildren each weekday. I pray for the oldest and the youngest on Monday, the second oldest and the second to the youngest on Tuesday and so on. This way, I touch the lives of two families in a special way every day.

I pray for my four children and their spouses in pairs on the weekends. This regular routine keeps me thinking about my whole family, not just the problems that come to my mind that day or seem to take precedence at the moment. Be sure to tell your grandkids you are praying for them. That's part of the blessing. When I told eight-year-old Patrick I prayed for him and his cousin Mark on Tuesday's, he said, "Good, Mark really needs it."

In *How to be a Good Grandparent*, Stephen and Janet Bly offer suggestions for how to pray for our grandchildren. They recommend prayer journals or notebooks (a steno-size book fits inside the back of your Bible) in which they record the names and birthdays of the grandchildren along with space to record the date and specific needs of the child. Some of the ways our prayers can include our grandchildren follow.

How to Pray for your Grandchildren

Choose a regular time to pray for each grandchild. You might like to use an inexpensive notebook to make a family prayer journal.

Write a grandchild's name at the top of the page, leaving a couple of pages in between.

Note the date (on the left side of the red line) and the prayer requests for the child.

What do you pray for?

The ordinary needs

their health and safety,
mental, physical, and spiritual growth,
strength to meet peer pressure,
courage to overcome temptations from drugs,
sex, etc.
Their specific needs, such as —
Josh is giving a science demonstration.
Kristi will have new braces.
Destiny is going skiing.
Laurie is taking the SATs.
Anthony didn't make the basketball team.
You'll probably also want to
Pray for their education
that their minds will be challenged,
for their teachers,
for a healthy, safe school environment,
that they will learn the greater lessons in life.
Pray for their spiritual development
that they will experience God's love,
that they will know the significance of prayer
in their own life.
that their church will be a rich resource of di-
rection and guidance,
that they will not resist the nudgings of the
Holy Spirit.
Pray for their careers.
Pray for their friends and future mates.
Pray for their wisdom...see Ephesians 1:17-19.
Let them know that you are praying for them.

♥x♥x♥x♥x♥x♥x♥x♥x♥

It is very important that you tell your grandchildren
you are praying for them. They will learn to rely on this
support and know you are always on their side. I heard
of a young woman who went to Europe with a couple of

her friends. Her grandmother told her that she would be praying for her especially while she was traveling. Later, the young woman related there were times she was tempted to go along with her peers to explore places and areas that she knew her grandmother would not consider wholesome. Thoughts of her grandmother's prayers reminded her (as if grandmother were looking over her shoulder) of her grandmother's faith and kept her away from risky and perhaps dangerous activities.

Since Biblical times a blessing from the patriarch has been a valued spiritual gift. **A blessing from a grandparent can have a deep impact on the lives of our children and grandchildren.** The blessing, a spoken word of our acceptance or a small ritual of our affirmation of love and loyalty, gives our dear ones (of all ages) that sense of belonging and security only a family can give. It's not hard to add a simple "bless you" once in awhile.

Marriage and family counselors Gary Smalley and John Trent asked people to describe specific ways they knew they had received a blessing. The responses in *The Gift of The Blessing* give grandparents suggestions for ways to bestow blessings on family members. "We went camping as a family," was a frequent response. "My parents really listened to me" and "They would take us out individually for a special birthday dinner" indicate the personal need for recognition. "We would all hold hands together when we said grace and when we finished we would squeeze the person's hand next to us three times, which stood for 'I love you.'" Grandmothers who plan old-fashioned sit-down dinners bestow blessings on the family and help the children develop table manners and common courtesy for one another.

Grandparents can be there too, when the kids have big, hard-to-answer questions. Even when they are very young and don't understand all the concepts (and do adults always understand everything spiritual?) we can plant the seeds for understanding in their minds and consciences. Her kindergarten-age grandson rushed in after school one day asking Grandma Rena how the earth began. Later she told me the teacher had told the children to ask their grandparents. Rena explained the Creation Story as she remembered it from her Sunday School days. Grandma Rena respected the teacher's wisdom in having the children learn the story of the beginning of the earth according to their own family's religious values and traditions.

Along with this thought of respecting one another's beliefs, a family story reminds me it is important that grandparents accept the young family's faith. The rancher parents left their first-born with the mother's mother while they were attending to some business in another part of the state. While the grandmother had the child in her care, she proceeded to have the baby boy baptized, without her Presbyterian son-in-law's permission, in her own Catholic faith. Needless to say, that grandmother never was very welcome in her daughter's home. A friend told me a similar story. Grandmother A had the older grandchild baptized in the Catholic Church one weekend and Grandmother B had the younger grandchild baptized in the Methodist Church the next weekend.

Dolores Curran, in *Traits of Healthy Families*, says that families need the same religious core in their lives although that does not mean they all have to belong to the same denomination and follow the same church theology. Having the same religious core means giving the same essential meaning to life and purpose for living.

One grandmother gives each of her children a Christmas gift of a daily meditation series. She hopes the families will have a feeling of togetherness since they all have the same inspirational reading, I have noticed that my grandchildren are often much more introspective and open to the "big" questions of life at bedtime or in the car on long trips.

A little book, *The Kids Book of Questions* has provided hours of conversation with my grandkids. It is a treasury of thought-provoking questions on ethics, fear, family problems, social pressures and friendship. Questions range from "If you could be invisible for a day, what would you do?" to "Do you believe in God? If not, why do you think so many people do? If so, what do you think God does all day?"

Grandkids catch on quickly if their grandparents rely on their faith to help them cope and keep them strong. Grandparents' faith in the future is demonstrated by their enthusiasm for life when they have positive attitudes and serve others in need. Grandchildren recognize the truth in the old saying, "Your walk speaks more loudly than your talk."

The National Center for Fathering in *Today's Father*, recommends "By the way you live, you'll be saying, 'My child, I've done my best to be a reliable reference point as you find your place in the world, but I'm going to make mistakes....'" The article says that a parent's duty is to introduce children "to a more stable, more reliable reference...a heavenly Father...."

Our family values our spiritual and geographical heritage. On a journey to Sweden with my daughter and cousin we visited the home parishes of five grandparents. It was thrilling to sit in the same pews where they sat 125 years ago and view the fonts where they were baptized. However, my grandparents probably didn't see the restored medieval wall paintings that we saw. Dating from the Eleventh and Twelfth Centuries when the Roman Catholic Church was the state church of Sweden, these unusual paintings were covered over in the Sixteen Century when King Gustav Vasa brought Lutheranism to Sweden from Germany. What a transformation that must have been for my ancestors to have their religious life altered so drastically. Realizing how the Swedish State Lutheran Church has been modified since my forebears time, I have a better understanding of the changes in our religious world today.

Another grandmother friend Elizabeth has also visited parishes of her heritage. She noted that a church, chapel, or cathedral of any antiquity probably has survived in spite of oppression and a succession of monarchs or leaders. Elizabeth said, "It gives us a new appreciation of the structure and stability, the diversity and tolerance which our Constitution tries to ensure."

All four of my grandparents were charter members of a little white frame church on a hilltop in South Dakota that they called the New Home Lutheran Church. That is where my family went every Sunday morning for 10 a.m. services. This church was also the hub of our community's social life as we participated in all the activities and groups. Members of the church were our neighbors and family. As the rural membership dwindled, the congregation moved to the nearby town of Mitchell. The original church building no longer exists but the site and the cemetery are commemorated with the founders' names on an historical marker set in place beside a new small tower that holds the old bell.

Before a recent family reunion, my daughter and a niece and their children were with me as we went back to the original site. Again I found it to be an emotional experience to study the historical marker and wander among the burial sites of four generations before me. The children romped through the high prairie grasses and read the old grave markers, exclaiming over the unusual ones. We had our pictures taken in front of the the children's Great-great-great-grandmother Ingrid's stone. And they giggled when I stood on my own burial plot between my parents' graves and that of the little brother who died before I was born.

Although the children were curious and a little embarrassed that I would talk of my own death, I felt comfort in their knowing where I would be buried. The New Home Cemetery is well cared for in an idyllic setting and my children and grandchildren will certainly have some of that same sense of family and generativity when they return.

Cousins Claire and Emilie stand on a strong religious heritage.

Kathleen Norris, poet-author of *Dakota: A Spiritual Geography*, moved from New York City to "the holy ground" of her childhood summers, her grandparents' home in Lemmon, South Dakota. She says she regained her spirituality as she dealt with her grandmother's household things, worked with people who knew her family and lived in the virtual isolation of life on the high plains of her heritage.

All of us are not lucky enough or perhaps wise enough to know the spiritual value of immersing ourselves in that baptism of our forefathers' and foremothers' spiritual geography or sense of place. But, Norris says "grandparents are doing theology" even as they welcome their grandchildren to wonderful family dinners in their warm, hospitable homes.

Arthur Kornhaber, M.D., wrote about the spiritual connection between grandparents and grandchildren. "How else can one explain the special nature of the grandparent-grandchild bond? Certainly not just physically, emotionally, or psychologically. There's got to be something more...and this something more (as 'unmedical' as it may seem to say) really seems to be spiritual in nature."

According to Kornhaber, "This spiritual dimension of the self not only contains love, wonder and joy but has the capacity to 'illuminate' and 'transform' the young and the old. Children seem to sense the spiritual qualities of older people and can transform what society generally sees as useless people into valuable elders." Children are often unaware of their ability to confer power and influence on the elderly. Kornhaber concludes, "But when love is present, children are blind to the wrinkles that so often blind everyone else."

In a recent sermon, our pastor told of an experience of spiritual bonding with his nine-month-old granddaughter. Traveling out of town, he was driving his son's four-wheel-drive with his wife beside him. Little Lauren, in her car seat, was happily babbling "in many languages I couldn't understand." Abruptly, the pastor was hit with extreme dizziness and waves of nausea, a terrible attack of Meniere's disease that had plagued him before. He pulled over to the side of the road and turned the wheel over to his wife, who had to concentrate on driving the unfamiliar vehicle.

The pastor got into the back seat beside Lauren and closed his eyes and tried to lie back to calm his dizziness. All of a sudden, he felt little Lauren's hand reaching out to his. She quietly held his hand and he felt a remarkable sense of comfort from his baby granddaughter. He described the experience as though he "walked through the valley" while his wife drove on to their son's home where he rested and recovered his composure.

The grandfather/minister compared his feelings to those of David the Psalmist as found in the Twenty-third Psalm, verse three, "He restores my soul." This grandfather realized that his tiny granddaughter had indeed touched him with a healing spirit, that day.

My grandmother friend, Jeannette, brought a copy of this verse to me from York Minster Cathedral in England and it continues to give me strength and courage to face the unknown. Minnie Louise Haskins, 1875-1957 wrote these words that King George VI used in his Christmas broadcast in 1939.

> I said to the Man who stood at the gate of the year, "Give me a light that I may tread safely into the unknown," and he replied, "Go out into the darkness and put your hand into the hand of God. That shall be to you better than light and safer than a known way."

As grandparents we often perceive a spiritual bond with our grandchildren. Many of us say that grandchildren give meaning and purpose to our lives, but we have a responsibility to share our understandings of the meaning and purpose of life. Not knowing what lies ahead for us and our dear ones makes us know that we must live as BEACONS — sharing our faith and courage with these young folks so close to our hearts.

Grandparents Are Security Blankets

God couldn't be everywhere
so He invented grandmothers.
— from a gift plaque

randparents have been around long enough to know that although the years go by and times change, somehow the troubles of the world remain much the same. Grandparents have been called deputy sheriffs and national guard who come when there are problems. They have also been identified as comforters and peacemakers. I consider myself and other grandparents as backup systems like the computer backup disk — in the background most of the time, but there if needed. A better description is that grandparents are someone you can rely on when there's change, when things are new and different or when your whole world falls apart. I like to say that grandparents are SECURITY BLANKETS.

What fun it was to see my granddaughter Carrie don a little plaid dress and wear ribbons in her hair as she played the role of Patty in her high school production of "You're a Good Man, Charlie Brown." The blanket that Linus held onto in the play made me think that grandparents are like security blankets. We wrap our grandchildren in an invisible cocoon of love and security even before we know they're real. Like a security blanket, grandparents offer comfort without confinement, courage without control, and carefree times without cost. Linus hangs onto his blanket when he feels most vulnerable but there are times he can let go and become independent. One of the toughest decisions for grandparents is to know when to intercede or when to intervene and become the security blanket and not just the pacifier that temporarily brings peace.

As I'm writing I'm listening to Verdi's *LaTraviatta* on public radio. Its story line and other operas such as *Madame Butterfly* as well as the TV soap operas have astounding similarities to true life stories. Family problems are found in all walks of life. Tragedy is so common we are hardly surprised at the sadness and trauma in our own neighborhood. Life is complicated and seems to be getting more so. Families need all the help that is available.

Parents of young teen parents have many troubles to resolve for themselves. These young grandparents are faced with their own thirty-something problems. One grandmother frantically tried to help her unmarried teenage daughter deliver the baby in the bathroom before its scheduled arrival while her thirteen-year-old son kept his cool and called 911. However, years later this grandmother maintains a strong bond with that granddaughter although the girl lives with her custodial father in another part of the country. The grandmother wants very much to keep in contact with that first granddaughter.

Family has taken on new definitions. Grandparents parent their own grandchildren while other elders delicately walk the fence trying to keep relationships with their adult children and grandchildren intact. Families fractured by divorce, desertion, drugs and addiction are especially vulnerable to problems between the generations. Intact families are not exempt from troubles either.

Teens and twenty-somethings are the first generation to grow up in homes where the majority of mothers worked. In the last twenty-five years the older third generation has not been included as family. Many grandparents of the '80s and '90s are young and still working or healthy and wealthy enough to travel, move to warmer climates and/or find new post-retirement activities. These are some of the explanations for the demise of the extended family.

Some grandparents feel they have raised their children and have no further responsibilities to help their young families. Young parents have such busy, complex lives as they try to juggle family life and careers with daycare, kids' school events, music lessons, sports activities and community involvement. I think it is most important that grandparents support young parents in their struggles. Connie worries about her grandson whose career-minded parents travel a lot and frequently leave him with different babysitters for long periods of time. It's hard in two-parent homes, but much harder in single-parent families. Providing back-up relief for the young parents can be your best duty.

Divorce often brings tensions for grandparents. Talking to my cousin on the telephone, Anne[*] asked about my book. "There's no joy in my grandparenting," she said. Neither of her adopted children has custody of her two grandchildren. Although her son insisted that grandparent visitation rights be included in his divorce action, Janie's mother frequently finds reasons not to

---

[*]Some names, identities and circumstances have been changed so as not to hurt or embarrass anyone.

cooperate. When eight-year-old Janie spends a once-a-month weekend with her, Anne tries to have her housework all done and plans her activities around Janie.

In between visits, Anne frequently writes notes, telling Janie she loves her and assuring her that she will always love her. She reminds her that when she was very small she lived with her and Nana (Anne's mother). Though Nana is gone now, Anne affirms that she will always be there and she can always come to her. The little girl has confided that her mother doesn't always tell the truth about the men she lives with. At this time Anne feels Janie is not neglected or has not been abused, yet this grandmother walks a tightrope hoping to keep the lines of communication open with her granddaughter and keeping watch for signs of trouble.

Anne hasn't seen her daughter's little boy in five years but she knows where he is and sends him little love notes and care packages. Her daughter Callie works in a large department store in a West Coast city. Callie's resources to fight for custody of her son do not compare with those of her ex-husband who has cut off all communication with her. Recently the nine-year-old sent his grandmother a thank-you note along with pictures of his school class. My cousin hopes the contacts with her grandchildren will provide them with a some sense of their family and perhaps the children will come back when they are old enough.

Grandparents who have to deal with their divorced children need to know that **divorce creates opportunities as well as dilemmas**. Usually, the maternal grandparents become more involved after a divorce and paternal grandparents see their grandchildren less often. Difficulties begin when the ex-daughter-in-law or ex-son-in-law becomes the opponent. All grandparents should focus on the grandchildren and not be as concerned with the problems of the parents. Many go the extra mile to seek the best for the children.

Jim G. and Char's ex-son-in-law has custody of their granddaughters who live with him and their paternal grandparents. The girls are with their mother two or three days a week. My friends count themselves lucky to have a good relationship with the other grandparents. Recently, both sets of grandparents celebrated a holiday together with the granddaughters, their father, uncle and aunt.

Char says the girls seem to thrive with the extra attention of four grandparents. Their grades are excellent, the needs not provided by their parents usually are supplied by the grandparents. The girls have a pretty good life knowing they are surrounded by a loving family — though their father and mother continue to disagree on clothes, boyfriends and other values. It takes a

lot of teamwork among the grandparents since there is little communication between the father and mother. The grandmothers worry together and carefully consider what they can do to make life better for their granddaughters. As the paternal grandmother explains, "We're not just a family, we're a co-op."

Esther's son and daughter-in-law have been divorced many years. She considers her daughter-in-law a remarkable person as she welcomed Esther into her home when she remarried. The granddaughters frequently spent weekends and vacations with Esther when they were small.

Building these relationships takes time and patience. Jill Krementz, in *How It Feels When Parents Divorce*, says that children of divorce suffer more than if a parent has died. When there is a divorce or the family is separated, the first thing to remember is that all children

GRANDMA ALWAYS SAYS FORGET THE SHEEP AND TALK TO THE SHEPHERD.

By BIL KEANE

REPRINTED WITH PERMISSION OF BIL KEANE, GRANDFATHER OF 8.

love their parents. Children are terrified about what will happen to them when their parents separate. This is the time when children need the stability and support of loving grandparents.

Social workers tell us children often do not want to be separated from their parents even when a parent has abused them. When an adult child and grandchildren are in crisis, grandparents must be courageous to keep their emotions in tact. We feel helpless, frustrated and oftentimes furious. But we can help if we focus our concerns on the children and continually help them know that we will never, ever desert them.

A friend's sister has demonstrated unrestrained kindness and compassion for her ex-daughter-in-law and unconditional love for her granddaughter. The young girl kept coming back to live with her grandmother because of the mother's alcohol addiction. When the granddaughter was worried and anxious about her mother, the grandmother and granddaughter together took food and blankets to seek out and care for the homeless mother on the street. The grandmother's hopes and dreams for her granddaughter have been realized. The young woman earned a college degree and is now in a successful military career.

Though we may feel frustrated and totally unable to understand a situation, we can help our grandchildren talk about and understand their feelings. We can listen and not deny their pain, **tell them it's all right to cry and feel angry; and help them find acceptabl**e ways to express their anger. We can tell them over and over that they will never be alone, that many people love and care for them — Grandma, Uncle John, Aunt Lucille, old Mrs. Brandon who lives next door, Miss Roberts the piano teacher. Children may not realize these folks who care for them keep them accountable, too. Grandma and Uncle John will also know when the kids get into trouble.

We can tell children their parents love them although they may not be able to love each other or live together. It helps to tell them we know they are strong and will survive; that they will be happy again someday. Talk and listen to them. Tell them they can always come to you with their problems. Reading children's books about divorce to kids empowers them with courage and strength. Ask at your public library for appropriate books.

The edges of bitterness and anger soften with time. Many relationships will heal if we don't say things we'll regret later or rush to burn our bridges behind us. John and Bonnie were not allowed contact with their only grandchild for many years but they sent messages and gifts to him in various ways. Now that he is older, he visits them and they love being together.

The custodial parent holds the key to when and if grandparents can see their grandchildren. In case of divorce that may mean grandparents have to bite their tongues, swallow their pride and bend over backwards to stay in good graces with the parents if that allows them to be in closer touch with their grandchildren.

In *Vital Speeches of the Day* Martha Dunagin Saunders reminds us that one of the most important three-word-phrases is "Maybe you're right." She says these three words can be disarming in almost any situation. There's nothing else to say and the argument stops. The one who speaks these important words is conceding the argument. That little "maybe" gently saves face for both.

Blended families is the term social scientists give to divorced and remarried families, although the blend isn't as easy as it appeared on TV's "Brady Bunch." Grandparenting step-grandchildren is not the same as grandparenting children who were born into the family. Step-grandchildren bring feelings from their other family units making instant loyalty to the new home difficult. Step-grandparents should be patient, slowly approaching as friends and waiting on the sidelines for the children to respond.

Ann Landers suggests that young children of divorce have suffered so many losses, they need all the love and support of elders that may be available. Grandparents, great-grandparents and step-grandparents can offer wonderful examples and experiences for children to learn about family life and values.

Jerry and Jack Schreur, in *Creative Grandparenting* suggest ways to grandparent when we're not sure how to react or respond.

1. Learn to live with your children's choices.
2. Don't punish your grandchildren or step-grandchildren for their parents' choices.
3. Accept your grandchildren the way they are.
4. Work for compromise.
5. Don't worry what others think.
6. Follow the Biblical mandate to love.

♥x♥x♥x♥x♥x♥x♥x♥x♥

If the step-grandchildren are adults, step-grandparents must consider that they have the maturity to choose an adult relationship with the step-grandparents. The association depends on the amount of contact that the new family unit has with the adult step-children. A loving close intergenerational friendship can result with respected elders and beloved youngers.

Lucinda's story is a model for "instant" step-grandparents. She taught elementary school children for many years before she married. Milton and his first wife enjoyed good times with their grandchildren before she died. Lucinda and Milton were married nearly ten years before Lucinda was widowed. She treasures how Milton's family accepts her and continues their relationship.

Lucinda's teaching days help her relate to her step-grandchildren.

Ten-year-old Andrew flew half-way across the country to spend two weeks with Lucinda. She wondered how she was going to keep him occupied until he discovered croquet. The two of them played croquet before breakfast, after breakfast, after lunch, in the cool of the afternoon and into the evening. An unexpected benefit for Lucinda was early recovery from carpal tunnel surgery. "I guess the exercise was really good for me," she said. Later when Andrew called to tell Lucinda he would appear with the children's chorus in the opera *Carmen* at the Kennedy Center, she assured him she would be there.

Lucinda also enjoys corresponding with her step-grandchildren. Although her granddaughter/college student frequently calls, she asked for letters to keep in touch while her college choir was on an international tour. On the choir's return, Lucinda got a phone call, "This is your granddaughter," the twenty-something said. Because the young woman had known her biological grandmother well, Lucinda counts her identification as grandmother especially endearing. Lucinda gracefully fills an empty space in her step-grandchildren's lives.

Another "instant" grandmother, Patricia, has found joy in step-great-grandparenting. A college professor, she retired and then married for the first time. It's a thrill for Patricia to feel connected to these little ones as she proudly shows pictures to her friends. Her family knows she has much love to share. Patricia and Lucinda have assumed roles as "beloved elders with beloved children."

Chosen and **adopted grandchildren and other non-biologically related grandchildren** also offer challenges to grandparents. Babies conceived by in vitro fertilization and sperm banks or those carried by surrogate mothers create new problems and feelings for traditional families. Interracial babies give the same sorrows and joys as "single race" babies but grandparents sense the prejudice and identity problems that lie ahead. Grandparents also struggle with emotions when their grandchildren live with their mothers and boyfriends or fathers and girlfriends.

Grandmother Ellen was glad to babysit for Chas while her son Bob and Linda were on their honeymoon. Linda is not the child's mother, but Ellen likes her and wants Chas to grow up with a family. Linda's two children, who live with them, are good kids and Ellen's support will help them all become a family.

Sometimes families evolve, not through planning, they just seem to happen. Grandma Jean was going on and on about her eighteen-month-old grandson BJ. She could hardly contain herself with the deep joy she was experiencing in her life with this little fellow. Then, she stopped short as if she had just remembered, "It's so strange, because he isn't even my biological grandchild."

Jean went on to say that BJ's mother, Lisa, was a "throw-a-way" teenager who came to their door asking to live with them. A few months earlier, Lisa had moved into their neighborhood and become friends with Jean's daughter. Jean and her husband, who is a minister, never doubted but that Lisa should be a part of their family. "It's funny," Jean said, "I almost think I can remember giving birth to Lisa. And my daughter feels the same way. She thinks she remembers being a little kid and starting to school with Lisa."

Now that Lisa is married and has BJ, that sound sense of family continues on down through the generations — not through the blood lines but through the wonder of love and caring. Sometimes it takes a miracle to make a family.

Much has been in the media about adopted children. Some adult adoptees who locate their birth parents after many years have positive responses but others find heartache. Sensational court cases that focus on adopted children being reclaimed by their birth parents are frightening to adoptive parents. Open adoption can also bring mixed emotions for the adoptive grandparents as well as the biological grandparents.

A grandmother friend Mary shared her feelings after her son and daughter-in-law chose open adoption. The adoptive parents were called to the hospital in the middle of the night and held the new baby before they left that morning. When Mary's son called he cautioned them not to tell anyone about the pending adoption. Maggie, the young mother, had actually chosen them to be the parents of her child, but she still had the option to change her mind. Later however, she signed the papers and the baby went home with his much relieved adoptive parents as arranged.

Grandmother Mary wondered what open adoption would be like. During the first year, Maggie and her mother made a few visits to see the baby. At the first holiday time, the birth grandfather came too, all bringing presents for the baby. Mary's family was surprised and pleased at the baby's extended birth family's concern. A young uncle sent a baseball trading card from his collection for the baby with the hope that the child will have an interest in sports.

Later Mary found out she knew Madeline and Mike, the baby's great-grandparents who live in another city. Mary wrote to Madeline expressing her deep appreciation for the gift of this precious baby who has made their family so happy.

Maggie's grandmother responded, "I'm...trying to put on paper my love and gratitude to all of you for making what could have been...sorrowful into a glorious celebration of friendship and families." The courageous great-grandmother concluded, "I surrender (this baby) gladly to your love and care — and then adopt all of you. What an astonishing development in our life's story."

Mary's story is continued with another poignant life episode. During the brief hospitalization and death of Mary's husband, the presence of this chosen child in the family gatherings offered a special sweet comfort in their time of sorrow.

Some grandchildren afford particular challenges for their grandparents. We elders think that the youth of our day were certainly not as bad as kids are today. This was the conviction expressed in the following paragraph:

> Our youths now love luxury. They have bad manners, contempt for authority, disrespect for older people. Children nowadays are tyrants. They no longer rise when their elders enter the room. They contradict their parents, chatter before company, gobble their food and tyrannize their teachers.

These thoughts are attributed to Socrates who lived 469-399 B.C. The Ancient Greeks were shocked by the actions of the younger generation. It seems things don't change much.

Other grandparents assumed the parental role for their fourteen-year-old grandson when their daughter literally brought him to their doorstep one Mother's Day. The grandson, I'll call Paul, was involved with a drinking crowd of older guys that could reflect on Paul's father's military career. With the family's future in jeopardy, Paul's parents saw no way out other than to remove him from the situation until the school term was over. It was fortunate that the transfer of Paul's family to another part of the country allowed Paul a new start in his teen years.

Paul's grandparents hesitated to accept this responsibility, but they wanted to help their daughter's family. He stayed on the farm for two months and his grandparents resumed their old regime of getting him to school on time and being involved in end-of-school activities. Paul pushed his grandparents as much as he dared — it was not easy for either of the three generations. In retrospect the grandparents are glad for the opportunity to model their family values and they admit to a better understanding of Paul and his peers as well as the problems their daughter and son-in-law face as parents in today's society.

Grandparents have to think what is best for everyone. It would be easy to "take over" a situation such as having Paul live with them. But there are other relationships to consider such as Paul's siblings and others in the extended family. **A family can't be re-built—it is construction in progress.** We have to look at the "Big Picture."

Chronic illnesses and conditions create heavy burdens for parents and grandparents when grandchildren have problems such as birth defects, retardation, autism, muscular dystrophy, visual or hearing impairments, mental illness, cerebral palsy, or cancer. Grandparents think of grandchildren as their future and hope and dream that their world will be a better place. Unfulfilled expectations cause grief and depression.

Grandma Chrys struggled with her own emotions when their suspicions were confirmed that little Betsy is a Downs Syndrome child. But, with their experience with other Downs Syndrome children and the wisdom they have gained through the years, Chrys and Bill have been able to accept Betsy as she is and to provide support to her parents. The extended family works together seeking information and ways to help Betsy grow to her highest potential.

In her grandparents' home, Betsy scrambles up the steps to the Teddy Bear Room where she plays with the bears and dollies — moving them from their beds and chairs jabbering all the time — much like any three-year-old. Betsy dearly loves "Barney" (the dinosaur) on television and videos.

Barney is the the only word, so far, that Betsy can say clearly, although her fingers sometimes fly as she learns to communicate in sign language. The little girl's progress is closely monitored as she attends regular classes. Though it's different, Chrys and Bill find much joy in grandparenting Betsy. This happy little girl has an engaging smile and mischievous ways that easily steals their hearts.

Although they struggle to fight resentment, embarrassment and loss of family pride when a grandchild is handicapped or disabled, grandparents tell me these experiences lead them to reorder their priorities. The special qualities of the child — the blind baby with beautiful blue eyes, the retarded toddler who never gives up — encourage grandparents to pick up the pieces of their broken dreams and move to higher ground.

Frequently Jane keeps her teen-age mentally retarded granddaughter for a few days so her twin sister can have some normalcy in her life. It's not the fun Jane had anticipated with twin granddaughters, but **she's learned to accept what she cannot change.** (This is the BIG adjustment.) Grandmother Julie often travels 300 miles to help care for her six-year-old granddaughter who is profoundly mentally and physically handicapped. Although Louann was a special education teacher, she's frustrated in not being able to help her autistic grandson. Sometimes all grandparents can do is provide encouragement for parents of children with special needs.

Grandparents who have experienced the death of a grandchild tell me they share many of the same emotions as the parents who lost the child. Grandparents sometimes feel guilty and blame one another even when these thoughts have no basis. Keeping the channels of communication open is the best comfort but it's hard to do. Talking helps diffuse anger and bitterness. Grandparents are urged to find a grief group where they can express their feelings. Hospitals, churches and funeral homes provide support groups that may vary in the way griefs are shared. Find a group where you feel comfortable talking about your loss and where you feel you are moving into new understandings.

I'm told that grandparents who know of aborted grandchildren often grieve and mourn for the loss of the child-to-be. These emotions may be mixed with relief and hope that their daughter or son will be able to move on to maturity and a better life. Most important is that the grief is recognized and worked through rather than denying that the abortion occurred and skipped over lightly.

Grandparents who are raising their grandchildren have been called "Silent Saviors." Maggie and Ron are in their seventies. Their twelve-year-old granddaughter has lived with them since she was three or four years old. Her mother, their only living child, cannot walk or talk since she tried to take her own life and has been in a nursing home the last several years. (The father is not in the picture.) Although finances are not the major consideration, Maggie and Ron find maintaining their energy level is a problem. Maggie recently underwent cancer surgery and radiation therapy. Having a vivacious, active pre-teen in the house is difficult and Maggie worries that the teenage schedule is going to get more complicated.

Maggie finds it hard to keep up — keeping their household running with food on the table and clothes for her growing granddaughter, visiting their daughter in the nursing home every day, driving her granddaughter to school and church activities, managing her own illness with doctor appointments and at the same time trying to sustain her long-time friendships as her main support. Ron is gentle and helpful doing his share but there's no time for him to relax or for the two of them to enjoy time together.

Maggie and Ron keep on keeping on. They worry about the future and have made plans for eventualities. But it's hard. "The worst thing," Maggie says, "is that I feel I've been robbed of being a grandmother. I have to be the mother."

Grandfather Don and Jerri got custody of two young grandsons when their mother was killed. Don's son was in the Navy and gratefully gave legal custody to his parents. Don and Jerri drove to Florida to pick them up when the youngest was nine months old and the other was about eighteen months old. Jerri put her plans on hold to complete graduate studies when the boys came to live with them. Don says his problems have not been as great as others — he has had a good job and was able to support the boys and his son has been cooperative. Don and Jerri are proud of these two high school graduates who grew up like their own sons and they are happily looking forward to less hectic retirement years.

Grandmother Dorothy is nearing eighty, but she finds herself parenting her teenage grandson. His parents had a bitter divorce several years ago and his mother and sisters moved to a new, safe location. It seemed best for Carl to live with his grandparents while he finished high school. Carl's grandfather, at age eighty, pretty much leaves the parenting to his wife. Carl is a good student and doesn't get into trouble. But,

Dorothy finds it hard to manage a household with these men of different generations and living different life-styles. When Carl leaves for college, Dorothy will remain involved, but hopes the everyday tensions will be relieved. The passage of time does ease the stress of differences.

A grandmother friend finds herself wishing the present was the past. Her youngest granddaughter, labeled gifted in her private school, became sexually involved with a much-loved teacher of another race in their school. The teacher was dismissed but not indicted since the girl would not testify against him. In an effort to "protect" the girl the administration suggested she not return to school. Now nearly eighteen years old, the girl has persisted with her education and has received her high school diploma through a GED program. The teacher has a new job in another part of the country and wants the girl to join him.

This grandmother suffers the loss of her expectations for her talented, charming granddaughter who has jeopardized her future. What can a grandmother do? She prays that her granddaughter will use good judgment and make wise decisions. Grandmother uses all means to keep communication lines open, never judging. She tells her granddaughter that she will always love her and be there for her. Grandmother hopes that with her family's support, this young woman will have a successful life.

Recruiting football players for the University of Nebraska-Lincoln has given Tom Osborne and his wife Nancy **a new appreciation for grandparents.** Nancy said, "Since the 1960s, Tom has traveled from coast to coast, visiting in the living rooms of every income level and race. In his pursuit of excellent student athletes, he has discovered that American families are changing. His visits used to involve two parents, then often one parent, and now often a grandparent filling the role of parent and sadly, sometimes, no parents. Grandparents, usually grandmothers, are playing a more and more important role in the lives of their grandchildren. (Grandparents substituting for parents probably needs a whole new book.) We ache for them because they are called upon to be parents twice, and are not getting a chance to experience the joy of **grand** parenting."

Grandparent support groups are meeting the need. In 1993, the Grandparent Information Center, supported by the American Association of Retired Persons (AARP) and the Brookdale Foundation Group, received more than 2,100 calls and requests for information in the first four months of operation. This response demonstrates the need for a link between grandparents and the resources that can help them care for their grandchildren.

Those attending an organizational meeting for a support network for grandparents raising their grandchildren heard sad and sometimes scary stories. Grandparents worry about their grandchildren when their sons and daughters or ex-sons-in-law or ex-daughters-in-law drift in and out of alcohol and drug addictions and from one marriage to another. The grandparents face dilemmas of how they can best help their grandchildren.

As grandparents in this group described their experiences, three major concerns came to light: 1) grandparents need to share the stories of their family troubles in a group, 2) they need information and assistance in working for changes in legal concerns and public policy regarding advocacy for children and 3) grandchildren who are being raised by their grandparents need a support network.

These grandparents deal with hurt and anger in their relationships with their adult children and their grandchildren. Many of the parents are involved with drug and alcohol addictions — often the grandparents went through similar situations in their own lives. The older parents feel guilt that their own children are not able to parent and that they made mistakes raising their own children.

Legal guardianship and adoption involves a lifetime commitment of finances, emotions and energy. Grandparents need to consider all aspects and possibilities before they assume the responsibilities for a time period that probably will exist for the rest of their lives.

Guardianship gives grandparents responsibilities without any guarantees that the child can stay with them. Many state laws direct the courts to return children to "intact families." Grandparents are not considered part of the "intact family" and children are often not consulted as to their choice for guardians.

I'm thinking how different it was seventy years ago, when the judge asked my Cousin Jim, who was eleven years old, who he wanted to live with after the death of his father — his mother who had abandoned him or his paternal grandparents. In the chapter, Grandparents are Kinkeepers, I told how Jim chose to live with his grandparents who were also my grandparents. Now in his 80s, Jim's successful life is a testimony to a young boy's wise decision.

Deanna has no legal custody or guardianship of her two grandsons although she has them every weekend. For the last five years she and her husband have purchased all the boys' clothing and school needs. Shelley became the adopted mother of her granddaughter and a widow in the same few months. She has to keep on working to support herself and her granddaughter. Getting legal custody cost her $12,000 and as the adopted mother she receives no Social Security or welfare support.

Some grandparents are literally the bridge or system to transport the children from one divorced parent to another. Grandma Beth picked up her grandsons after their visitation at her daughter's home and returned them to the custody of her ex-son-in-law. Beth visited the children's schools and learned more about the school/custodial parent situation. She became acquainted with the children's teachers and gained information that helped her daughter, the mother of her grandsons, regain custody.

Guardianships, custody and other legal issues are discussed in the last chapters of Arthur Kornhaber's *Grandparent Power!* More than four million grandparents are raising their grandchildren. Legal issues are a vital, continuing topic. Kornhaber urges building strong relationships even before our adult children are married to diffuse conflict if divorce or other problems occur.

Before one even thinks about going to court, you should consider mediation. Most intergenerational family problems are temporary, according to Kornhaber, and time and counseling can soften the blows. Going to court results in adversarial action determining "winners" and "losers" in a family conflict which often means escalation of bitter feelings.

Mediation brings feuding families together in a neutral setting to discuss their grievances in non-confrontational ways. Family members may act as the go-betweens although it's difficult to be objective when you know the histories of all involved. Professional mediators have been trained to bring opposing parties to reconciliation. Negotiation and mediation are much better than court action to bring about healing of family wounds. Family service agencies, family counselors, or clergy can help you find a mediator. Check your local Yellow Pages for mediative therapists.

Weigh carefully your decision to go to court. A judge's ruling cannot bring about love and consideration. For more information read Kornhaber's *Grandpar-*

ent Power! in which he thoroughly reviews court procedures, what to expect from an attorney and how the best interest of the child is demonstrated.

Families are fractured and frayed from the complex problems and tough issues common in our culture. More than anyone in the family, grandparents have the responsibility and obligation to be the comforting presence in the life of their grandchild. Grandparents need to be SECURITY BLANKETS.

♥x♥x♥x♥x♥x♥x♥x♥x♥

*One of the greatest joys is
to have grandchildren fight over your lap.*
— Anonymous

Grandparents Are Sages

Even if I knew the world would end tomorrow,
I would still plant my little apple tree today.
— Martin Luther

Grandparents are SAGES...**and wise elders, revered ones, advisers, counselors, mentors, teachers and VIPs.** Simply by having lived longer, grandparents acquire experience and knowledge that make up the good sense we call wisdom. The grandparents I'm telling about in this chapter are VIPs — Very Important People. They are grandparents *extraordinarie* — Grandparents Plus — for the impact and influence they have on their own grandchildren as well as future generations.

Grandmother Blye has sixty-five grandchildren at the last count and no one can doubt that she has had plenty of experience and undoubtedly gained much wisdom. A marketing firm found Blye "the grandmother in Nebraska who has the most grandchildren," for a car rental company's magazine ad. When the ad agency people came to Nebraska to take her picture, Blye was all dressed up in her Sunday best. The photographers insisted she looked too classy for a grandmother with that many grandchildren. Blye went to her closet and chose another dress that still didn't suit. Finally after several clothing changes, she was pictured primly in her navy blue skirt, a plain white blouse and a red sweater, that she usually wore around the farm at choretime.

Sitting on a straight, antique chair holding photographs of her grandchildren, Blye portrayed a Thanksgiving matriarch. The ad copy suggested something like "If you go over the river and through the wood to Grandmother Blye's house, you will have to share the turkey with her 65 grandchildren."

When the West Coast-based advertising people were finished, they offered Blye a check for $100. She hesitated and then politely said she thought she was worth more than that. She figured that the agency had spent a lot of money flying three people to Nebraska the night before. They had stayed in a nice motel and eaten a good dinner as well as breakfast that day. Blye continued on. If a New York model had been asked to change her clothes as many times as she had, Blye supposed the model would have gotten more than $100 for her modelling fee. The rest of the story is that Grandmother Blye received her just compensation. A wise grandmother indeed who knew her own value as an individual.

Grandmother Waunda raised her own granddaughter and now adores her great-grandsons Luke and Jesse. But in addition, Waunda is the unofficial "church grandmother" for she has been the main caregiver in the church nursery for many years being available at four different worship hours every Sunday.

Pastor Bliss says that many young families attend St. Mark's because they know their little ones will be safe and comfortable in the nursery. He should know because his own toddler granddaughter insists on going to see Waunda when she visits. "Graduates" of Waunda's groups frequently stop in to say hi and some of the junior high helpers first came as babies. Grandmother Waunda is a VIP to many children who have known her loving care.

Grandmother Marguerite has nineteen grandchildren to make her proud and keep her and Grandpa Ed busy going to events of all kinds. In the space of three days they attended Little Gil's kindergarten graduation, Matt's high school graduation, and they caught their first glimpse of Madelyn who was 24 hours old. And the three grandchildren live in three different states. Marguerite was pleased to be honored for her service to her church by the young people by the latest confirmation class whom she had taught. Besides having taught the CCD classes for many years, she's the substitute organist, visits the nursing home and assists in many other ways. But another award from her former students of 52 years ago, really surprised her. The two women were visiting an aunt in Marguerite's community and presented her a favorite teacher award. Students don't forget Marguerite and her grandchildren won't forget her either.

Grandmother Betty loves to be with her own grandchildren in other parts of Nebraska but this retired home economics teacher can't get enough of kids, horses and sewing. She saw a need for the Salt Creek Wranglers 4-H Club and thought she could help. Before the horses are shown in competition, they must be groomed to look their shiniest best. Keeping the horses' tails clean before the horse shows is a problem. Cloth bags to cover the tails are available commercially, but Betty thought they were too expensive. With the help of her young friend Melissa, she plugged in her sewing machine and whipped up a sample which proved to be just what was needed. Betty and Melissa went into production and the 4-H Wranglers sold the tail bags at a nominal fee which garnered $200 for the club fund.

Betty doesn't leave her sewing machine unattended very long. When she heard that several cloth remnants had been donated to the Family Resource Center, she set to work designing and making book bags. The bags were distributed at a "back-to-school" ice cream social to encourage school kids to **read and enjoy books.**

Grandmother Violet has sewed for her grandchildren since before they were born. She's still making costumes and beautiful dresses for her granddaughters who must be the best-dressed teens in their schools. But, layettes for newborns and quilts for babies are really her specialty. My grandbabies loved her patchwork flannel quilts and inspired my daughter to make them for their new baby friends.

Violet doesn't stop with sewing for her own, she stocks the Church Closet with layettes for the poor and homeless families. Discount stores like KMart and Wal-Mart give her sleepers and children's clothing that cannot be sold. She fixes the zippers, repairs seams and mends tears to make the clothing like new and helps distribute them through the Closet at Trinity Lutheran.

Grandmother Chrys is a crafty grandmother who often shares her projects with her own brood of grandchildren. However, she decorated a bright-colored baseball cap with buttons of all kinds for Diane, the daughter of good friends, who was undergoing cancer treatment. Diane's cap made such a hit with other cancer patients that Chrys made more.

When I heard of my friend's project, I gave her a small tin of odds and ends from my button accumulation. Chrys thanked me profusely for my meager contribution but her affirmation of our mutual feelings touched me more —"Since you shared your family jewels, that makes us real sisters now, doesn't it?"

Other friends and neighbors heard of the cap project and have also contributed buttons. She received grocery sacks full of little white buttons. Can you imagine how many little white buttons there are in one fifteen pound sack? Chrys takes the buttons, caps, needle and thread along whenever she anticipates a few minutes of waiting time. She continues to make caps in memory of Diane.

A pastor and other friends help distribute Diane's Caps that are as bright as "Joseph's Technicolor Raincoat." The fluorescent tangerine, stop-sign-yellow, brilliant fuschia, vivid turquoise, deep purple and every other color caps spread sunshine and rainbows throughout the hospitals and homes struck by cancer.

Someone said, "Love is like a loaf of bread and two fishes. It's never enough until you give it away."

Grandmother Jackie, another retired teacher and principal, often spends time with her own five grandchildren who live in other states but she has taken to tutoring and grandmothering the granddaughter of her friend. Mary, age twelve, is being raised by her grandparents and Mary's grandmother feels she and her granddaughter have been deprived of their grand-relationship. Jackie fills in the gaps by helping Mary with her school work and doing grandmotherly things together.

Grandma Sylvia and Grandpa Bill keep in close touch with their eight grandchildren although none of them live in their same town. When fourteen-year-old Mark came to their door and asked if they would be his 4-H foster grandparents, they couldn't turn him down. He was a busy young man with school and helping his folks on the farm, but he stopped in every once in awhile. Sylvia and Bill were interview subjects for school assignments and he remembered them with gifts. Now that he is teaching in California, they still hear from him.

Each winter Sylvia and Bill go to Texas and live in a retirement community where they miss their grandchildren and other young people. Sylvia met Kathleen and her mother while shopping and wrote a note asking if they could be Kathleen's foster grandparents. Kathleen is in the middle of ten children in the family and her only other grandparent lives in Australia. She feels special to have grandparents nearby. Bill spends his days fishing and Kathleen often comes over to share his catch. In school she made a ceramic fish that she gave to them. They taught her to play dominoes and she taught Bill card tricks. Kathleen and her "grandparents" are learning about each other as they share their lives across the generations.

Many grandparents have special stories but one of the most remarkable is **Grandmother Arlette Schweitzer of Aberdeen, South Dakota.** Arlette was the surrogate mother for her twin grandchildren. The moment she delivered the twins, she turned her maternal duties over to her daughter and assumed the role of grandmother. A public speaker these days, she tells her audiences that she would do it all over if the need arose.

In our town the **Kiwanis Grandpas** regularly make connections with children in elementary schools. Some of the men have no grandchildren and find this affiliation enriches their lives. Under the auspices of the Lincoln Area Agency on Aging, the **LINK (Lincoln's Intergenerational Network for Kids)** program gets children and elders together. Some friendships that began with second and third graders meeting nursing home residents have lasted on throughout high school.

Notable grandparents have words of wisdom to share with all of us. John Rosemond, who writes extensively in newspaper columns and magazines about parenting and families, became a grandfather for the first time in 1995 with the arrival of Jack Henry. In his first month of grandparenthood, he concluded that grandparents have to let the new parents make their own mistakes in order to learn parenting skills. He says, "God made our children before He gave them to us. All we have to do is take reasonably good care of them and everything will fall into it's proper place."

Jack Henry's arrival prompted Rosemond to reread Dr. Spock. He discovered the favorite baby doctor gave much the same advice that affirms and validates grandparents' wisdom. Spock counsels, "Love and enjoy your child for what he is...and forget about the qualities he doesn't have."

Art Linkletter, a grandparent and great-grandparent, mirrors these thoughts. (I'm not sure who came first, Spock or Linkletter) Linkletter says the best gift to a grandchild is unconditional love —"...I love you, I'm going to love you, no matter what you do."

Generativity versus Stagnation

Most of us become grandparents during "middlescence," the stage of the life cycle Psychologist Erik Erikson describes as the time of Generativity versus Stagnation. In the midst of transitions and adjustments to growing older we begin to ask, "What have I done with my life? What have I contributed? How can I make the world a better place to live?" People with the sense of generativity are hopeful for the future — concerned what happens after they are gone. If we focus on our regrets and give up hope, we cease to share. Our thoughts turn inward and our life stagnates. Grandparents with a sense of generativity direct their lives toward giving and look forward with hope to make life better for future generations. These grandparents keep on growing and investing their time to help their grandchildren and other youth to grow up to be successful people.

Grandfather Don Clifton, CEO of The Gallup Organization, usually finds time in between his worldwide travels to spend one hour a week with each one of his grandchildren. The entrepreneur uses the same work-place philosophy of "one-on-one positive relationships" with his grandchildren. Clifton spends his weekly visit with each of his grandchildren doing whatever the child wants to do.

In their book, *Soar With Your Strengths*, Clifton, with co-author Paula Nelson, identifies his management agenda which describes a positive work relationship as investing in another person by doing things for that person's own good without consideration of self-reward. Each person working at Gallup has his own personal "board of directors"— co-workers who help define goals and provide support for the individual.

Clifton makes it his business to know each of his grandchildren as individuals — to be on the child's board of directors. In our short talk he described their strengths and their potential in true grandfatherly fash-ion. "Jonathon has an excellent sense of humor. Jackie shows talent for playing the clarinet. Mark is the most competitive kid I've seen. Lauren's talent is with horses. Meredith loves to practice telling stories. Michael is physically active...very effusive." Both Clifton grand-parents encourage and cheer for each grandchild. "It's thrilling to respond to their interests. We spend time with them, doing what they want to do. We give them drops to fill their buckets...."

It was the 1960s when I first heard Dr. Clifton give his popular motivational talk about "The Bucket and the Dipper." (Perhaps Meredith inherited her grandfather's storytelling talent.) The message is that we each carry a bucket of self-esteem and we each also have a dipper. When you fill another's bucket with your dipper, you raise the level of their self-esteem making them feel good about themselves and the level in your bucket is also increased — you feel better about yourself, too. However, if you dip into someone else's bucket lowering their self-esteem, the level in your bucket also goes down.

Dr. Clifton has been filling the buckets of young people long before he became a grandfather. As a University of Nebraska professor he started the Nebraska Human Resources Institute; a project ahead of its time. Forty years later, University students interact and mentor high school students in a leadership development program. Clifton left the University to found Selection Research, Inc. (SRI), a management-consulting company which in 1988 acquired and retained the name of The Gallup Organization.

I asked Grandfather Clifton about his own grandparents. His maternal grandmother lived in a little house on their same ranch in Northern Nebraska. She gave him total acceptance; she'd say "Whatever you do is OK." His grandmother was always glad to see him, never a nitpicker or nagger.

When he was fifteen or sixteen years old and could drive a car, Clifton drove for his grandmother running errands here and there. He remembers his grandmother even encouraged him to drive faster. And one time at her urging grandmother and grandson drove through a a small creek bed — and neither ever told his parents.

Clifton has never questioned his grandmother's unconditional love. I don't question that any grandparent's unconditional love and acceptance will make a difference.

The title, "Sacred places whisper voices of ancestors" drew my attention to an article by **Professor Paul A. Johnsgard**, who teaches biological sciences at the University of Nebraska-Lincoln. Johnsgard took his granddaughter to one of his "sacred places"— a Pawnee County hillside. He wanted her to witness with him the annual spring dance-mating ritual of prairie chickens.

To ensure the birds would put on their display without too much delay, he took along a tape player and a recording that had been made on the same hill. Coincidentally he noted the tape was recorded April 7, 1970 — twenty-five years ago. Johnsgard realized that he was using the recorded voices of the great-great-great grandparents to call the present generation of male prairie chickens.

Johnsgard wrote, "This powerful realization, that ancestral voices might pass down through subsequent generations and influence them, even though the birds themselves are now dead, made me think of how the same might apply to me." The professor explained that the "voices" of his paternal and maternal grandfathers spoke to him through their values and heritage. His mother's love for English literature and the legacy of natural history books were passed down to inspire Johnsgard's career choice.

He continued, "Thus, I can personally show my granddaughter some of my own sacred places in Nebraska and introduce her to one of my very own special spring rituals. There may be better reasons for viewing an April sunrise while sitting on an obscure hilltop in eastern Nebraska, but I can't think of one."

Grandmother Governor Kay Orr walked through the halls of Nebraska's Capitol Building pushing a stroller with two other young grandsons beside her. They were passing time as they waited for the boys' mother to finish an errand. The little guys recognized their grandmother's portrait hanging in the halls with all the other former governors. And they delighted in knowing about the door to the elevator on the lower level that went directly to the Governor's Office above them.

Grandmother Kay, in her teaching role, reminded the boys that Ben Nelson is now the governor of our state and Bill Clinton is the president of our nation. The little troupe continued their leisurely pace and Grandma reviewed their lessons. Five-year-old Alex said, "I know Mr. Clinton is our president, but I forget whose office is in this building. Is it Rush's?"

Although, the little boy was aware of his daddy's wont of listening to Rush Limbaugh, his newly acquired political knowledge left Alex a little confused. He is just a little boy who likes to be with his Grandma. It doesn't matter to him that she was once the first woman governor of Nebraska.

Kay Orr became a grandmother for the first time with Taylor's arrival soon after she became governor. Kay shared her hopes for all children's future as a poignant open letter to Taylor. "You're just beginning a long life, Taylor...All of us, your parents and grandparents and relatives, have put together the elements of a whole identity for you to inherit and absorb. Some you can't escape...Some you'll probably want to reject...And some, I hope, you'll cherish because they represent the solid values of a family that cares...."

Grandma Orr went on to emphasize her concern "to make people aware of our American heritage...you'll undoubtedly hear about your responsibilities as a citizen long before you're old enough...to vote...We're a patriotic bunch. We've been blessed...we'll make sure you know exactly why."

Grandmother Orr advised Taylor about values. "We, as a family, hope to instill in you our spiritual values...We want you to learn to be a responsible and caring person...in all your relationships...It's a tradition with us that each succeeding generation has reached a little further, aimed a little higher, than the last...."

Summing up the family philosophy with her new grandson, she said, "I'll probably remind your mother of how we used to say, 'You can second guess us, argue and disagree, but you can't question our motives. What we do is done for you because we love you.'"

That's how Governor Kay Orr wants her grandchildren to remember her — as their grandmother who loves them. Bill and Kay Orr enjoy taking their grandchildren to their Iowa lake cabin. The children's favorite beach toys are old plastic kitchen utensils — measuring cups, sieves, bowls, spoons and spatulas. In fact, through the year the children love to scour the junk stores for "new" and better beach paraphernalia. Though Kay Orr's journey through life has given her national recognition, her hopes and dreams for future generations are pure and simple grandmother thoughts.

Grandfather Tom and Grandmother Nancy Osborne are Very Important People to grandson Will although Dr. Tom may be better known as the head football coach of the Nebraska Cornhuskers, the 1994 National Football Champions. Tom told a group of us that it was tough to be a head football coach, but that it was also hard to be a grandfather. To illustrate he told a story.

It seems Will asked his grandpa to make a noise like a frog. Tom said that was something he'd never been asked before, but he said he croaked out some sounds and Will seemed to be satisfied and went off to play with a little friend. Tom was listening in on the little kids' conversation and he heard Will tell his friend that he was going to DisneyWorld. Tom hadn't heard about this, so later he asked Will when they were going. "Pretty soon," his grandson said. "Mommy said that we're going to DisneyWorld just as soon as Grandpa croaks."

Grandpa and Grandma Osborne are also recognized as extra-ordinary people by many others. In 1995, they were awarded the prestigious Father Flanagan Award for Service to Youth. Past recipients include

Mother Teresa, Michael Jordan, Bob Hope, Danny Thomas and others. Father Val J. Peter, Boys Town executive director said, "Although national championships are wonderful, Tom and Nancy were chosen back in November (before the national championship) for this award...They have been outstanding role models to athletes, families and youth alike."

Having raised their own three children, the Osbornes continue to act as surrogate parents to 130 eighteen- to twenty-two-year-old football players. Nancy said she sometimes feels like they are building a bunch of characters instead of building character. She compared raising kids to cultivating a garden or field, if it is not tended the weeds grow. Because the Osbornes regard children as our most precious resource they are concerned for all the untended fields of children and their influence on our country's future.

About five years ago, the Osbornes started TEAM-MATES, a program in the public schools. "At-risk" junior high students are identified and paired with mentors from the University of Nebraska Athletic Department. The students are provided tutoring, job shadowing and someone who demonstrates a caring concern for them. If the kids stay with the program and finish high school, they will receive scholarships from the Lincoln Public Schools Foundation for schooling after graduation.

This year TEAMMATES graduated their first class. Three-fourths of those who started graduated and will go on to college. The Osbornes began the program with their personal gifts and have inspired other donors to give funds to the Volunteers in Schools and Ventures in Partnerships programs in Lincoln, Nebraska.

In a talk, Dr. Tom explained the motivation for his and Nancy's generosity with words attributed to Mother Teresa, "Unless a life is lived for others, it's not worthwhile."

Intergenerational Activities

We all are part of humankind and all of us make mistakes and errors in judgment. But, as grandparents we share the responsibility to promote understanding among the generations and to strive for a better future for our grandchildren.

The Older Americans Act of 1965 produced Adopt-A-Grandparent and Foster Grandparent programs. Since then, senior citizens have joined with the younger generations in numerous projects and organizations. Intergenerational programming has spread throughout educational, religious, community and government circles.

Generations United, a Washington-based organization, was formed in 1986 to "promote cross-generational understanding and cooperative action." More than a hundred organizations adhere to the mission to extend the good aspects of grandparenting to all communities and society. Here in the Midwest, I know of two state organizations, Kansas Intergenerational Network (KIN) and NE\Generations United (Nebraska) that are dynamic in their support of intergenerational programming.

Not all of us are remarkable grandparents as described in this chapter who so actively demonstrate the impact grandparenting and intergenerational activities can have on society. However, we must make our effort now, for our grandchildren and generations of children to come.

My brother Paul Carlson compiled a series of writings over the years and his introductory remarks seem especially appropriate here.

Someone has said "'People — that's what life is all about.' Our relationships with others are important to them but they are also important to us. Where do we learn about people? Where do we learn to love? We need to be in a loving relationship to experience the joy of it and above all we need to work at it."

In his last Christmas letter before he died Paul included the following rhyme. He and his wife Violet had found it inscribed on an ancient clock in Chester Cathedral, in Chester, England.

When as a child I laughed and wept,
Time crept.
When as a youth I waxed more bold,
Time strolled.
When I became a full grown man,
Time ran.
When older still I daily grew,
Time few.
When I shall find in passing on,
Time gone.

♥x♥x♥x♥x♥x♥x♥x♥x♥

GrandCHILDREN Make A Difference

Grandchildren are God's reward for growing old.
— an old proverb

f you've read this far and have learned your lessons, you know how important you are to your grandchildren. You know that we wear many different hats as we interact with our grandkids — we are kinkeepers, magicians, playmates, heroes, bridgebuilders, beacons, cheerleaders, security blankets and sages. Now, I want to consider how important grandchildren are to grandparents — how **Grandchildren make a difference in our lives.**

They make us laugh and smile. We each have our favorite grandchild story that we are willing to share with our friends at the drop of a hat. Roy Blount, Jr., wrote about his four-and-a-half-month-old grandson Jesse Roy in *New Choices for Retirement Living*. "I realize there are lots of grandchildren around, but he is the most delightful one I have ever met. He looks at his feet and laughs and laughs...My feet are all right, but they are not, to me, a reliable source of amusement."

Children are a reliable source of amusement and faith in the future. My friend tells me her friend's very

blonde daughter married a very black man and they
have a beautiful little girl named Faith. One day Faith's
mother told her they were going to visit her grandma.
Little Faith asked, "Do you mean my pink grandma or
my brown grandma?"

Another grandma learned more about children's
perceptions one day as she walked her dog in the neighborhood. A little boy playing nearby struck up a conversation and joined her. He was very comfortable walking
with her and told her how much she reminded him of
his own grandmother. "You talk like my grandma and
you smell like her and you even look like her," he said.
Shirley was pleased and flattered, realizing the little African-American boy didn't consider her obviously white
Anglo-Saxon heritage.

Grandma Idonna listened as four-year-old Katie
talked about her preschool friends — she was especially
fascinated with Jeremy. This was her first-time acquaintance with an African-American child. About the same
time, grandmother and granddaughter were looking at
the ultrasound sonogram of Katie's yet-to-be-born
brother. Katie chattered away, about the black and white
picture, "I guess he's going to be the same color as
Jeremy." Grandmother didn't see the need for any further explanation for her "color-blind" little granddaughter.

Yes, just being with our grandkids makes us smile.
I think it has something to do with the fact that neither
grandparents or grandchildren had anything to do with
bringing about our relationship so we have no precon-
ceived ideas. Perhaps they remind us of our own children or even of ourselves.

Grandchildren make us proud. America's favorite
inspirational writer Marjorie Holmes reflected on becoming a grandmother. "*Grandmother*...I will grasp and
savor the true beauty of that word — its grandeur and

its glory. To be a grandmother. What a compliment. May I live up to it."

Nebraska's State Poet Bill Kloefkorn wrote poetry before his first grandchild was born but he always said he was not going to be like all the other grandparents he knew. He certainly was never going to write any poetry about *his* grandchildren. However, after Michelle was born Kloefkorn noticed that his grandchild wasn't like all his other friends' grandchildren. She was a lot cuter, a lot smarter and had a lot more personality. So, of course he had to write about her. *My Granddaughter, Age 3, Tells Me The Story Of The Wizard Of Oz* may not be his first poem about Michelle, but I like it. It begins:

> There is a brain, she says,
> right here, she says,
> pointing to the front of her head,
> but the Scarecrow
> doesn't have one yet,
> not until the end of the story.

♥x♥x♥x♥x♥x♥x♥x♥x♥

Like other grandparents, my grandchildren make me proud so I have stories to tell, too. Eleven-year-old Michael is a great golfer and he also likes people. He golfs with retirees who have been playing for years. He calls the mayor and other city fathers by their first names — not because he's discourteous but because they are his friends.

Phillip, fifteen, has made me proud playing the clarinet in the San Luis Obispo Youth Symphony. Named to county and state honor bands, concert bands and orchestras, Phil has added a new feather to his cap. After one semester of keyboard or typing, he's a whiz typing between 65 and 80 words per minute, when 35 words per minute is the minimum requirement to pass the course! Since he has mastered fingering on the clarinet, he has become an expert on the keyboard.

At the beginning of the school year, Patrick's teacher asked his class what second graders would like to learn. Since no one else responded, Patrick raised his hand, "I really want to learn more about Einstein's theory of relativity, you know about E=MC squared." I never have understood Einstein's theory and I don't know if the second grade class learned it either.

Nana Soni had great training before she became a grandmother as the most significant caregiver for my granddaughters Carrie and Emilie. She used to listen to my "bragging" stories about my grandkids and now she tells me "proud" stories about the four grandchildren she and Grandpa Dean have.

Their three granddaughters moved back with their parents to the Midwest after four or five years living in Vermont and Connecticut. Seven-year-old Megan pondered some of the differences between living on the East Coast and the Midwest. "Nebraska doesn't have Sundays," she said. Her grandmother couldn't understand Megan's thinking until she went on, "We don't go to Sunday School and church like we did back in Connecticut." Soni was quick to explain to me that the young family had just not decided on a church home yet.

Yes, grandchildren can make us proud, perhaps we're proud that our own adult children are modeling the values we feel are important. Grandson Patrick received a new sled the winter he was three. But nature didn't cooperate and when the sledding hill was still brown, his mother suggested that he pray for snow. That's when his sister Claire spoke up. "That wouldn't be right," the four-year-old gently scolded her mother. "It might interfere with somebody else's prayers." Parents and grandparents often discover that real wisdom comes out of the "mouths of babes."

Grandchildren keep us young. That's what most grandparents say. That isn't just a trite saying they heard *their* grandparents say. When you are involved with your grandchildren, caring for them once in a while, trying to keep up with them, you realize again why God gave grandchildren to young parents.

Most of us only remember our grandparents as being old. You have heard the story of the new grandfather whose only complaint was that it now meant he was married to a grandmother. Some people feel that becoming a grandparent automatically places them in the "old" category. I was an adult before I realized that old does not consist of the number of years you have lived. As a parish visitor, I was amazed that Olga at ninety-years was more vital and alive than fifty-six-year-old George who just sat and complained.

It's hard to remember that no matter how old grandparents are, our grandchildren consider us old. Eight-year-old Katie had been begging to take the family's coveted autographed Nebraska football to school for Show and Tell. Her mother, fearful for the football's security, finally agreed if Katie's grandpa would go along. At school Katie introduced her subject,. "Holding our Nebraska football, is Mr. Fortune, my sixty-nine-year-old grayhaired grandpa. Notice how much gray hair he has."

Another of the Fortunes' granddaughters, thirteen-year-old Amy, gave them another left-handed vote of confidence. "I'm sure glad that you're not disabled so you can drive us around and take us places," she told her active, but tired, grandparents.

Three-year-old Jason doesn't consider age to be of any consequence. Grandpa Lou and his family were eating at a restaurant and Grandma Elizabeth was taking pictures. Lou noticed that his grandson seated in a booster seat beside him appeared to be as tall as his grandfather. Lou remarked that since they seemed to be the same height, people wouldn't be able to tell them apart. "Grandpa, I'll just tell them that you are the one with the wrinkles," Jason said.

Grandchildren sometimes have solutions for aging grandparents. After a bath, three-and-a-half-year-old Christopher asked Grandma Dorothy to help him out of the tub. She was down on her knees and said she couldn't do that since her knees creaked, but he was a big boy and could get out by himself. Christopher hopped out of the tub and put his arm around her shoulder and said, "Grandma, maybe I can get you one of those sticks with a curved handle on it."

Walter M. Boritz, M.D., of Stanford University, says the "disuse syndrome" is responsible for physical weakening, mental decline and emotional deterioration such as depression. Psychologist Erik Erikson said almost the same thing when he described generativity versus stagnation. Unless we continue to grow and give to others, we lose our vigor and vitality. As we relate to our grandchildren and respond to them, they do keep us young and healthy.

Arthur Kornhaber reminds us that being involved with our grandchildren gives us good feelings, "Every psychiatrist and psychologist can tell you that happiness is a direct result of a positive emotional relationships to others." Furthermore positive relationships help us live longer — we are more immune to disease and better able to cope with problems of all kinds.

Grandchildren give us an excuse to shop. The discount stores have beautiful, brightly colored new sporting equipment: balls of every size and shape for every purpose (you can always play with a ball), rackets, bats, hockey sticks, golf gear, fishing tackle and biking para-

phernalia. Much of it is for the safety of the child —
something grandparents always have in mind.

Grandmothers satisfy their shopping urges buying
clothes for young granddaughters. (I've learned that a
gift certificate is a better idea for teenagers.) What a joy
for grandma to buy the dolls she never had. (Their little
girls may not be into dolls — however, they will make
grandma happy if the dolls she gave them are displayed
in their rooms when grandma comes to visit.)

Grandchildren are the perfect excuse for us to buy
stuff we couldn't afford for our own children or we
won't buy for ourselves. We can use the grandkids to
justify buying a computer with all those cool video
games so we can experience "virtual reality." (Isn't a life
of sixty-five-plus years enough virtual reality?) Grandparents rationalize the grandchildren need something to
do when they come to visit. Sometimes adult kids get
hooked on solitaire, too.

Grandchildren help grandparents remember.
Someone said elephants and grandchildren never forget.
The kids will remind us of the promises we made — that
we said we'd take them fishing or to the park — even
though it's raining cats and dogs. We dust off the cob-
webs trying to remember where we hid the candy and
treats we bought when we learned the grandkids were
coming. Or where did we put that book or game we
bought at the summer clearance sale to give little Horace
for his birthday?

Grandchildren also help us remember that we once
were kids. We remember that an ice cream cone only
cost five or ten cents or that a movie was a quarter or
fifty-cents. Maybe we should remember how bored we
were when our grandpa talked about walking through
six feet of snow five miles to school. Your grandchild
may enjoy your recollections of taking Grandpa to the
Sadie Hawkins Day dance or how about the time you

went hunting and your rifle put a hole in the floorboard of the old Chevy. Some of our memories really don't impress our grandchildren very much unless it relates directly to their life now.

Matthew had a Show and Tell story that topped all the others in his kindergarten class. He told about his great-great-grandfather who had died in the Civil War—which was absolutely true. However, Matthew said that he died in a plane crash. He had his eras a little mixed up, but it is understandable since Matt's father was in the Air Force and the table conversation about a recent plane accident had undoubtedly led to the confusion. At any rate, Matthew is proud of his heritage.

A little boy named Austin was also a good story-teller. As he retold the story of "Jack and the Beanstalk" the tale went on and on getting more involved. Finally, Austin's father said, "I think you're making that up." Austin admitted it, "Yep, you're right. That's what I do best."

Sometimes, it's okay to embellish or embroider your memories to make the story a little better. Mark Twain said, "When I was young I could remember anything whether it happened or not." And Elizabeth Stone suggested in *Black Sheep and Kissing Cousins*, "Attention to the stories' actual truth is never the family's most compelling consideration. Encouraging belief is."

Grandchildren keep us honest. Emilie was about five when she and her dad met us on campus before a Nebraska football game. After our lunch together, I did my grandmotherly duty and stopped with Emilie at the ladies' rest room. We waited in a long line for what seemed like a long time. Then, when we were ready to leave, I grabbed Emmie's hand trying to hurry out the door. She strongly resisited, "But, Grandma, we didn't even wash our hands." So we backtracked past a long line of smiling women and washed our hands and dried them carefully. Emmie still wants to do the right thing. She's persistent and does good work.

Grandchildren keep their eye on the speedometer even when you don't realize it. When the county fair entrance fee is free for children six and under, you can be sure that Tommy will loudly proclaim to the world that he just had his seventh birthday. Elementary children are usually strong law and order conformists. They play by the rules. Poppa better not cheat at checkers.

It also occurred to me that grandchildren remind us to be honest with ourselves and take care of the world, for our grandchildren will be paying our Social Security and the National Debt that we incur here and now.

Grandchildren keep us out of the ruts of life. They constantly challenge us with new ideas garnered from their affair with technology. If you want to learn how to program your VCR, just ask your grandchild. You can learn to use a computer by asking your five-year-old granddaughter. Learn baseball statistics from your grandson who has a trunkful of baseball trading cards. Find out what's going on in their heads by asking your teenage grandchild the words on their latest pop CD. In fact, you can learn a lot from your grandchildren — ask them about rollerblading, soccer, pogs and hockey. Ask them about recycling. Our schools have done a great job teaching our grandchildren how to protect the environment.

Grandchildren remind us to think of others. I never met Carrie's other grandmother. I hadn't thought much about her until the Decoration Day when Carrie was five. That was the first time she went to the cemetery where her other grandmother was buried. My daughter explained her Grandma Evelyn had been very sick and died before Carrie was born, and that we decorate the graves of the people we love on Memorial Day. Carrie said, "I've made lots of cards and stuff for

Grandma Orr, but I've never made anything for my other Grandma." So our little flaxen-haired dolly went to work.

The next day at the cemetery, Doug planted the geraniums and Cyndi helped Carrie fix the fragile paper project from Vacation Bible School and secure the card to the grave marker. Later Cyndi told me about the greeting card that Carrie made. Much like the many love notes I was accustomed to getting, it was covered with hearts and rainbows and Carrie's childish handwriting.

I thought of Carrie's other grandma and sensed a kinship with this granddaughter we share. I imagined how she perceived that quiet country scene with the red blooms, the squished yellow tissue butterfly and Carrie's messages.

DEAR GRANDMA,
I LOVE YOU.
PLEASE GET WELL
SOON.
        LOVE, CARRIE

When we know and understand our grandchildren, we see the paper boy who misses the front step in a different light. The little girl who picks our first tulip for her grandmother isn't an ornery brat. The tired mother with a hungry baby in the grocery checkout line has our sympathy. Because our grandchildren are in the car we don't yell at the slow driver ahead of us. Because of our grandchildren, we watch our language when we miss the nail and hit our thumb. We worry about the homeless kids who exist without the abundant trappings of our own grandchildren. We're troubled with the TV images of children in war ravaged countries. We reach a little deeper into our pockets to make a difference for others not as fortunate as we are.

Grandchildren give purpose and appreciation for our lives. When that first grandchild arrives our thoughts of family take on new meaning. Grandmother Charlotte glorifies her brand new grandmother role. "He recognizes my voice and looks in my direction when I'm talking. My heart just melts when Tyler looks at me. I'll do anything for that baby." A widowed grandmother glowed "He lights up my life." "They make me feel as though I'm the greatest person in the world," a ranch grandmother said. We live life more fully and joyfully. The little things become more important. "I love the expressions in their eyes and watching them eat ice cream," was one grandfather's response. Grandparents love the toothless grins of babies, the sticky hugs and kisses.

Being a grandparent fosters appreciation for the happy times and not having the responsibility. One grandmother said, "I can love 'em and leave 'em. I can enjoy them but I don't have to accept responsibility for their material needs, their education, or their social needs." Grandparents love to see the grandkids come to visit and they like to see them go home. One grandmother told me, "I can send them home, tired and cranky, with their dirty clothes." Our grandchildren enhance our lives with a fresh outlook; we see the world through new glasses. Grandchildren teach us the quiet satisfaction that comes from living for somebody other than ourselves.

> **Kids are 27% of our population,
> but they are 100% of our future.**
>
> — Michael Josephson

❤✗❤✗❤✗❤✗❤✗❤✗❤✗❤✗❤

The promise of our future — step-great-grandchild, Nicholas Paul.

Grandchildren are the promise for our future. Sitting next to an elderly couple at a Lied Center concert, I learned that the couple had just returned to the Midwest following a winter in Arizona. "We came back early this year since we had a new great-granddaughter who was born in Omaha." I asked if a great-grandchild is different than a grandchild. My seatmate said, "Each great-grandchild is a bonus...you don't know how much longer you have, and you want to stay around and see them grow up. I hope to still be here for our fourth great-grandchild who is due in August."

Grandchildren give us continuity as they link us to our days as parents and our days as children. As we look at our grandkids we learn about ourselves — we find out how our children turn out as parents. We also are reminded of our memories of our grandparents or the stories we have heard about them. Grandparents often say grandchildren give them a second chance. They remember the mistakes they made as parents and regard the new generation as an opportunity to do things better. Grandchildren link us to the future as well.

Author Alma Bond cherishes "...each day I am permitted to memorize my children's faces and touch the hearts of my grandchildren. I can find solace in these arrows into the future. To be a grandparent is to pierce the bull's-eye of eternity."

Grandchildren energize and empower us. We do things with our grandchildren we never thought we could do. Grandmother Marjorie N., age seventy-three canoed down the Niobrara River with her twelve-year-old grandson Bobby. And they participated with a night time "Star Party" at Merritt Reservoir. Since Marjorie had learned astronomy as a World War II pilot trainer, this was a chance for her to share other experiences with her grandson.

Another day she and Bobby joined a group going down the river in huge inner tubes lashed together. "We pushed off and traversed the thirteen miles without incident. We were first on the river and first out at the bridge," Marjorie said. When they were back at camp, she overheard the ultimate compliment from a youngster. "Boy that grandmother of Bobby's is one tough old bird."

Mary Costello dedicated one "Over the coffee cup" column to the rewards and gifts of grandparenting — especially babies. "Babies are wonderfully accepting and completely non-judgemental. They make everyone feel strong, worthwhile and successful." When she changes her nine-month-old grandson, he looks at her as if to say it was far and away...the fastest, the most comfortable, the most efficient diaper change he ever encountered. "He makes me believe I'm a wonderful pants changer. And sometimes I need that."

Grandmothers tax their physical abilities to keep up with the kids and Grandpa will tackle any project his granddaughter suggests. Grandpa Bud has to call his granddaughter long distance to find out the results of the science project he helped her develop.

Grandchildren are the lasting batteries that keep us going like the Energizer Rabbit that keeps going and going and going. Why do grandparents have all this pep and fervor for grandparenting? Most grandparents say they love being with their grandchildren and watching them grow. They like the sound of their voices, the enthusiasm they have for life, the excitement they bring when they come to visit.

Grandparents give us unconditional love. To hear our grandchildren turn the tables and brag about us is another joy. A greeting card that pictures a bumper sticker that says "Ask me about my grandparents" becomes a treasure. Children who are loved know how to give love in return. Just as we try to show them our kindest, warmest, happiest selves, especially when they are alone with us, they give back their best selves and are mannerly, obedient and charming.

It was a junior high composition assignment that prompted Grandson Mark's essay on Grandparents. He summed up his thoughts very well.

> Grandparents
>
> Grandparents are special because thier always thinking of you. There nice, always writing you letters and sending you presents. Their smart funny and always telling stories. If you think your parents are nice they probubly got it from there granparents.
>
> Mark Orr, 13

♥X♥X♥X♥X♥X♥X♥X♥X♥

Ruth Goode explains, "They (grandchildren) praise our skills, accommodate to our oddities, excuse our shortcomings and as they get older they even enjoy our eccentricities." Grandchildren accept us as we are without criticism or trying to change us. They are more approving than anyone else in our lives has ever been — not our parents, our siblings, spouse, friends and even our grown children.

The media chastised Nebraska's Tom Osborne after the Cornhuskers lost a disappointing football game to Iowa State but his little grandson helped him gain a new perspective on the situation. Tom said, "Grandson William doesn't care if we won or not. He still loves me."

Sometimes we think we do too much for our grandkids but there's no way to measure the ways they enrich our lives — simply by being. The delight we have in seeing them grow and flower cannot be expressed or understood except by other grandparents. As parents, we couldn't stand back and enjoy our children because we were too close — we were responsible. But with the arrival of our children's children our lives glow with new purpose and meaning. Grandchildren light up our life at that time when life gets too serious.

Take time this very moment to thank the Lord for your grandchildren. May you always know THE JOY OF GRANDPARENTING and that GRANDCHILDREN DO MAKE A DIFFERENCE.

Resources

A Grandparent's Journal. Running Press Book Publishers, 125 South 22nd St. Philadelphia, PA, 1985.

Amble, Becky L. *Love From Grandma*. Minneapolis: Future Focus Press, 1994.

Bly, Stephen and Janet Bly. *How to Be A Good Grandparent*. Chicago: Moody Press, 1990.

Boucher, Therese M. *Spiritual Grandparenting: Bringing Our Grandchildren to God*. New York: Crossroad, 1991.

Cherlin, Andrew J., and Frank F. Furstenberg, Jr. *The New American Grandparent*. New York: Basic Books, Inc., 1986.

Clark, Karen Henry, "The Trouble with Teen-Agers" in *Readers' Digest*, July 1993.

Clifton, Donald O. and Paula Nelson. *Soar With Your Strengths*. New York: Delacorte Press, 1992.

Costello, Mary. "Over the Coffee Cup" copyrighted 1990 by Costello & Associates. Published by *Lincoln SunPapers* (Lincoln, Nebraska, 1990)

"Cultivating a Spiritual Connection With Your Kids" in *Today's Father*, The National Center for Fathering. (Shawnee Mission, KS 66204)

Curran, Dolores. *Traits of Healthy Families*, Winston Press Minneapolis, MN, 1983.

Daily Guideposts. Vols. 1988 through 1995. Guideposts Associates, Inc., Carmel, NY 10512.

Dodson, Fitzhugh. *How to Grandparent*. New York: Harper Row, 1981.

Endicott, Irene M. *Grandparenting by Grace*. Nashville: Broadman and Holman, 1994.

Farber, Norma. *How Does It Feel To Be Old?* Berkeley: Creative Arts, 1981.

Fox, Mem. *Wilfrid Gordon McDonald Partridge*. Brooklyn: Kane Miller, 1985.

Goode, Ruth. *A Book for Grandmothers*. New York: McGraw Hill, 1976.

"Grandparents-Grandchildren: A Spiritual Connection?" in Vital Connections: *The Grandparenting Newsletter*, Fall 1990 (Lake Placid, NY 12946)

Greer, Kate. "The Meeting Place." *New Choices for the Best Years*. May 1991 (Retirement Living Publishing Co., Inc., subsidary of Reader's Digest Association, Inc. NY, NY).

Gutowski, Carolyn. *Grandparents are Forever*. New York: Paulist Press, 1994.

Haley, Alex. "Grandparents can do more..." From a speech to a group of teachers in Sacramento, California, circa 1980.

Haskins, Minnie Louise. "I said to the Man..." Used by King George VI in Christmas broadcast 1939. Publ. by Tim Tilley, Ltd., 157 Chiltonham Road, Bristol B56, England 5RR.

Hellmich, Nanci. *USA TODAY*. "COVER STORY Relationship forms lasting bond of love." November 24, 1993, The Gannett Co., Inc.

Johnsgard, Paul A., "Sacred places whisper voices of ancestors," *Lincoln Journal-Star*, April 22, 1995, Lincoln, Nebraska.

Kornhaber, Arthur, M.D., and Sondra Forsyth. *Grandparent Power!* New York: Crown, 1994.

Kornhaber, Arthur, M.D., and Kenneth Woodward *Grandparents/Grandchildren: The Vital Connection*. New York: Doubleday, 1981.

Kornhaber, Arthur, M.D. *Between Parents and Grandparents*. New York: St. Martin's, 1986.

Krementz, Jill. *How It Feels When Parents Divorce*. (New York: Knopf), 1984.

LaPlaca, Annette. *Grandparents Have All the Fun*. Wheaton: Harold Shaw, 1992.

LeShan, Eda. *Grandparents: A Special Kind of Love*. New York: Macmillan, 1984

LeShan, Eda. *Grandparenting in a Changing World*. New York: Newmarket, 1993.

Leipzig, Judith and Maryann Brinley. "Family Dinners: Time For Conversations." *Good Housekeeping*. March 1995 (Hearst Corporation New York, NY 10019)

Lott, Joyce Greenberg, "Here Come the Grandmothers" in *MS*. March/April 1993.

Meier, Paul and Paul Thigpen, "Family Tapestry," *Aspire*, December 1994/January 1995, Nashville, TN.

MIT Museum, 265 Massachusetts Avenue, Cambridge, MA 02139.

Modern-day heroes, by Susan Campbell of *The Hartford Courant*, *The Lincoln Star*, Jan. 31, 1995, Journal-Star Printing, Lincoln, NE.

More Heart Warmers. Compiled by Helen Lesman. Lighten Up Enterprises, Minneapolis, MN, 1986.

Norris, Kathleen. *Dakota: A Spiritual Geography*. (Houghton Mifflin Company New York, NY), 1993.

Orr, Clarice A., *The Grandparent/Grandchild Relationship: The Grandparents' Perspective*, Lincoln, Nebraska: University of Nebraska, 1986).

Orr, Kay, "Some quiet time with Taylor," *The Lincoln Star*, July 9, 1988 (Lincoln, Nebraska).

Peel, Kathy. "A Family Affair." *A Better Tomorrow*, March/April 1995, Royal Magazine Group, Thomas Nelson, Nashville, TN.

Reader's Digest, anecdote, February, 1995, contributed by Walter Irvine, p. 109.

Rogers, Dale Evans with Carole C. Carlson. *Grandparents Can*, 1983.

Rosemond, John. "Granddad will let kids make own mistakes." *Lincoln Journal-Star*, April 16, 1995, Journal-Star Printing Co., Lincoln, Nebraska.

Saunders, Martha Dunagin, "3 Words That Can Change Your Life," from "Vital Speeches of the Day" in *Readers' Digest*, Pleasantville, NY, Dec. 1994.

Schreur, Jerry and Jack, with Judy and Leslie Schreur *Creative Grandparenting*. Grand Rapids, MI: Discovery House, 1992.

Seuss, Dr. and A. S. Geisel. *You're Only Old Once!* New York: Random House, 1986.

Shedd, Charlie W. *Then God Created Grandparents and It Was Very Good*. Garden City, NY: Doubleday, 1976

Smalley, Gary and John Trent, *The Gift of The Blessing*. Nashville: Thomas Nelson, 1993.

Stillman, Peter R. *Families Writing*. Writer's Digest Books Cincinnati, OH, 1989

Stock, Gregory. *The Kids' Book of Questions*. Workman Publishing, New York, 1988.

Stone, Elizabeth. *Black Sheep and Kissing Cousins. New York Times*, 1988.

Stoop, Jan and Betty Southard. *The Grandmother Book*. Nashville: Thomas Nelson, 1993.

Swindoll, Chuck. *The Strong Family*. Portland: Multnomah, 1991.

Warren, Ramona. *Loving Legacy*. Nashville: Thomas Nelson, 1993.

Weaver, Frances. *The Girls With The Grandmother Faces*. Midlife Musings, Saratoga Springs, NY 1994.

Wild, Margaret. *Our Granny*. New York: Ticknor and Fields, 1994.

Wyse, Lois. *Funny, You Don't Look Like a Grandmother*. New York: Crown, 1989.

Wyse, Lois. *Grandchildren are so much fun, I should have had them first*. New York: Crown, 1992.

Other

Designs by Kelley, (314) 926-2702 in the St. Louis area.

Klutz Press, 2121 Stauton Court, Palo Alto, CA 94306, has a free Flying Apparatus Catalogue describing all the Klutz books that tell kids how to have fun with old fashioned entertainments. The books come complete with harmonicas, boomerangs, yo-yos, marbles, jacks and juggling stuff. Klutz books are also available in gift shops, drugstores and bookstores.

The quotation "Our youths now love luxury..." has been attributed to Socrates although the date of the writing — 4 B.C. — indicates it was probably written by Isocrates, a student of Socrates. RQ, a library reference periodical, suggests the original work can be found in the ancient writings, Areopagiticus, page 135 and Antidosis, page 343.

Good Life Tour and Coach, 8200 Fletcher Avenue, Lincoln, NE 68507 Toll Free (800) 233-0404 or in (402) 467-2900

FUN TOURS, P.O. Box 94904, Lincoln, NE 68509 (402) 475-3956,

For information about personal 800-numbers with AT&T call 1-800-327-9700 or with Sprint call 1-800-877-4000.

Michael Josephson founded the Josephson Institute in honor of his parents. For more information contact Joseph and Edna Josephson Institute of Ethics, 4640 Admiralty Way, Suite 1001, Marina del Rey, California 90292-6610 (310) 306 1868.

The Grandparent Information Center is located at AARP Headquarters 601 E. Street, N.W. 'Washington, D.C. You may telephone the Center at (202) 434-2296 weekdays from 9 a.m. to 5 p.m. EST. This is not a toll-free number. You will hear a recording asking you to leave a message and your telephone number. Center staff will respond to your call. This procedure minimizes the long-distance charges for the caller.

Grandparents' Day was first proclaimed National Grandparents' Day in 1978 by President Jimmy Carter having been conceived by Marion McQuade of Oak Hill, West Virginia. Mrs. McQuade "Wanted to make people more aware of the knowledge and experience" which is lost when our grandparents die.

Gramma's Graphics, Inc., 20 Birling Gap, Fairport, NY 14450-3916 (Sun Print kit for making heirloom quilts and wallhangings.).

Grandparent Education

Grandparent Classes: Becoming a Better Grandparent and Achieving
Grandparent Potential
Shirley and Robert Strom
Arizona State University
Tempe, AZ 85287-0611

Grandparents Little Dividends
Young Grandparents Clubs
Sunie Levin P.O. Box 1143
Shawnee Mission, KS 66207

Joy of Grandparenting
Clarice Carlson Orr
7100 Old Post Road, #20
Lincoln, NE 68506

Grandparent Support Groups

AARP Grandparent Information Center
601 E. Street NW
Washington, DC 20049
(202) 434-2296

Grandparenting by Grace Support Groups
Discipleship & Development Dept.
Sunday School Board, Southern Baptist Convention
127 9th Ave. N.
Nashville, TN 37234
(615) 251-2280

Grandparents Care
Marty Smith

344 S. Columbine Circle
Englewood, CO 80110

Gramps—Granparents Rights Advocacy Group
Pat and Jack Slorah
1225 North Florida Ave.
Tarpon Springs, FL 34689

Grandchildren's Rights to Grandparents
237 S. Catherine
LaGrange, IL 60525

Grandparents as Parents (GAP)
Sylvie de Toledo
Psychiatric Clinic for Youth
2801 Atlantic Ave.
Long Beach, CA 90801

Grandparents Raising Grandchildren
Barbara Kirkland
P.O. Box 104
Colleyville, TX 76034

Grandparents'-Grandchildren's Rights
Lee and Lucille Sumpter
5728 Bayonne Ave
Haslett, MI 48840

Grandparents Raising Grandchildren
Carol Ann Dyas
129 N. 10th, Room 333
Lincoln, NE 68508

Grandparents Rights Organization
richard S. Victor
555 S. Woodward Ave. #600
Birminghan, MI 48009

Grandparents United for Children's rights
Ethel Dunn
137 Larkin St.
Madison, MI 53705

Orphaned Grandparents Association of Edmonton
The Family Centre
9912-106 St. 3rd Floor
Edmonton, Alberta, CN T5K 1C5

ROCKING, Inc. (Raising Our Children's Kids)
P.O. Box 96
Niles, MI 49120

Scarsdale Family Counseling Center
Edith Engle, Marjoire Slavin

405 Harwood Building
Scarsdale, NY 10583
*For a support group for grandparents raising their grandchildren in your area, contact your local Area Agency on Aging.

Intergenerational Programs

Center for Family Education
Dr. Helene Block
Oakton Commnity College
7701 N. Lincoln
Skokie, IL 60077

GenerationsTogether
Dr. Sallie Newman
600A Thackery Hall
University of Pittsburgh
Pittsburgh, PA 15260

Generations United
Tess Scannell
440 First St. NW # 310
Washington, DC 20515

Kansas Intergenerational Network (KIN)
Jean Miller
P.O. Box 47054
Topeka, KS 66647
(913) 266-2491

Menninger Child Care Center
Kathleen Leon, Director
5301 West Seventh
Topeka, KS 66606

National Intergenerational Week
Fred Ramstedt
350 Arballo Dr. 10-J
San Francisco, CA 94132

Nebraska/Generations United
Carol Ann Dyas
129 North 10th, Room 333
Lincoln, NE 68508

St. Francis Academy
Mary Lou Calhoun
509 East Elm Street
Salina, KS 67401

About the Author

Clarice Orr returned to college to obtain her master's degree — in grandmothering — because she wanted to be a good grandparent. For her human development thesis, she surveyed 270 grandparents concluding, "People want to have a good relationship with their grandchildren and extended families." The "professional grandmother" finished her master's in gerontology in time for the arrival of her tenth grandchild.

The retired University of Nebraska editor writes and talks about family issues combining her grandparenting research with warm, endearing stories of grandparents and grandchildren. A published author, she has given slide-talks, workshops and seminars to national and state meetings and conferences on grandparenting, aging, intergenerational programming and building strong families.

Clarice Carlson Orr grew up on a farm near Mitchell, South Dakota and moved to Lincoln, Nebraska, with her husband and four children in 1956. The ten Orr grandchildren — 9 to 26 years old — two step-grandchildren and three step-great-grandchildren live in Nebraska, California and Ohio.

For more information or scheduling a workshop or seminar, call Mrs. Orr at (402) 483-0652.

Index